What Really Matters in Ministry

What Really Matters in Ministry

Profiling Pastoral Success in Flourishing Churches

Darius Salter

BAKER BOOK HOUSE
Grand Rapids, Michigan 49516

Library of Congress Cataloging-in-Publication Data

Salter, Darius, 1947–
    What really matters in ministry: profiling pastoral success in flourishing
churches/ Darius Salter: foreword by Robert Coleman.
        p.   cm.
    Includes bibliographical references.
    ISBN 0-8010-8300-1
    1. Pastoral theology. 2. Success. I. Title.
BV4011.S29 1990
253' .2—dc20   89-38803
                                                                    CIP

The King James Version is used as the basis for this study. Other transla-
tions used are the New International Version (NIV) and the Revised Standard
Version (RSV).

Contents

9904

Foreword

The perceptive Edward McKendree Bounds once commented that "the church is looking for better methods, but God is looking for better men."

Discomforting as the observation may be, I suspect that it hits closer to the mark than we like to admit, especially in church-growth discussions. What is also apparent, we tend to define accomplishment in terms of visible results, not intangible spiritual reality.

For fear of being misunderstood, let me affirm that nothing is wrong in seeking to enlarge ministry outreach. Indeed, our Lord has taught us to be diligent in seeking to reach more people with the gospel, careful not to let the children of this world outdo the saints in astute stewardship of resources. It is imperative that the church find ways to bring everyone to Christ.

In the effort to be effective, however, let us not confuse measurable statistics with the values of heaven. There are differences, you know. The treasures of earth may have little resemblance to those things which moth or rust cannot corrupt nor thieves break through and steal.

That is why this book by Darius Salter is so timely. It comes to grips with an issue easily dismissed in the hustle and bustle activity of the contemporary church. After all, what really matters in ministerial service?

Approaching an answer to this question, the author takes a representative profile of distinguished American pastors—men deeply admired for their pastoral work—and probes how their ministries measure up to biblical standards of success. In the process, we are made aware that success must be seen in the light of eternity; Christian character is more to be desired than a winsome personality; and only that work done for the praise of God alone can endure.

To get its meaning focused, he brings us to consider the cross on which the Prince of Glory died. There finally is the measure of ministry, and painful as it may be, there each of us must come to terms with our own aspirations of success.

Reading this account has been for me a sobering, yet very rewarding, exercise, and I commend it to you with the same expectation.

Robert E. Coleman

Acknowledgments

Allow me to express appreciation to several people. First of all are the pastors who took time to fill out the questionnaire. Many of them wrote encouraging notes, and several went beyond the call of duty in providing insights for which the survey instrument did not call. Second, my thanks to the denominations that provided permission and information which enabled me to target the men who were leading them in numerical growth. Third, I express appreciation to my employer, Western Evangelical Seminary, for providing a financial grant and relief from my teaching load, both of which have been enabling factors in this research.

Jim Field did much of the data processing for the project. I thank him for the expert assistance he has rendered, not only in providing averages and correlations but invaluable advice along the way. Joseph Coleson and Donald Hohensee did careful reviews of the manuscript and offered many helpful suggestions that have been incorporated into it.

Jerry Sather has provided inestimable assistance in the project. For the last two years he has served as my research fellow, doing word processing and collecting data. His contribution has been invaluable.

Also existing in the background are my co-workers at Western Evangelical Seminary, my patient, long-suffering students, and the many mentors who have shaped me in past academic enterprises. I especially thank Thomas

Oden of Drew University who has been a model of scholarly research and who offered encouragement and insight for doing revisionary work on the project. I appreciate Robert Coleman, my former professor and continuing friend, for writing the foreword.

Last, but not least, are the churches where I was pastor, in which and for which I at times did a poor job of defining success. This book may be nothing more than an illusion, a fantasy that I could return to those hallowed sanctuaries and undo some mistakes of those early years. Better yet is the conviction and hope that what has been can become what ought to be for many of us in ministry. I am convinced that the men we will examine in this book will provide a standard for excellence in ministry.

Introduction

Western Evangelical Seminary
A Graduate School of Theology
and Christian Ministries

Rev. John Doe
123 First Street
Anywhere, USA

Dear Rev. Doe:

This is an invitation to lunch. I trust that
five dollars will still buy a noonday light meal
in your town. Obviously I cannot personally join
you except via the twenty-minute survey
enclosed. Please find a nook in your favorite
food franchise and visit with me via this questionnaire. If this is impossible, please complete the survey and spend the five dollars for
something else.

You have come to my attention as the kind of
pastor about which thousands of other pastors
need to know more. Your response will be very
much appreciated, since I am surveying a very
select number of "successful" pastors. The
information from you and others will be the substance of a book, *What Really Matters in
Ministry: Profiling Pastoral Success in
Flourishing Churches.* You will be enabling me
and hopefully thousands of others to discover
what makes a pastor successful. If you cannot
complete the survey within the next month, kind-
ly destroy the five-dollar check.

Your quick and honest answers on this inventory
will be deeply appreciated. I am

Gratefully yours.

Darius L. Salter
Chair, Pastoral Theology

11

The procedure was quite simple. One hundred men were surveyed, men who have been pastors of rapidly growing churches over the last several years and have brought their present charges to over five hundred in Sunday morning attendance. One hundred eighty questionnaires were sent out to churches representing nineteen denominations. These pastors were carefully chosen through recommendation by others, denominational information, and through such general works as Elmer Towns and John Vaughn's *The Complete Book of Church Growth*. Many of the churches I have personally visited, as I have made it a practice for some years to visit the "growingest, goingest, happeningest" church in a given town on a given Sunday.

I purposely have not included pastors who have some unusual fame through television or authorship. My intention was not to discover men with unique or unusual abilities heading megachurches. Very few of the men have anything close to national fame, but they are individuals who are leading growing, thriving churches, the average size of which has 1650 in attendance on Sunday morning.

We may also legitimately ask how one hundred men can provide a fair sampling, and the question is well taken. First of all, I was not looking for a sampling; neither was I attempting to provide an average or comparison description. I carefully selected the people who already fit a prescribed profile: pastor of a numerically growing church of over five hundred. It took a good deal of time and energy to find 180 people who fit this description. I then wrote to these busy people what I thought was a unique letter. It worked; a group of 112 responded, which was then pared down to one hundred. It is my conviction that those one hundred responses told me more than would one thousand responses out of ten thousand random questionnaires.

I write both out of conviction and need. Every student who graduates from our seminary as well as a multitude of other ministerial schools across the United States, more or less wants to be a success. I stand as a step, however minor, within that preparation process. If I am going to be a legitimate step, I need to have a better understanding of pastoral success and how it is achieved. My reader could legitimately begin by asking me to define the word *success*. But allow me to beg off for now, and say that defining pastoral success is the overt purpose of the book. We will tread cautiously.

The odyssey will not be linear or straightforward enough for some, at least those who want immediate answers with all paradoxes removed. Success in pastoring is not uniformly or universally defined. Definition will demand patience and at times discomfort.

Such discomfort reminds me of a friend who answered an advertisement in the newspaper for an able-bodied seaman to sail with the owner of a twenty-five-foot sloop to a distant Pacific island. The owner of the boat was somewhat cranky and spent most of the time in the hold of the vessel. He complained if my friend, who did most of the steering and navigating, got the boat off keel, which caused the owner discomfort. Because of having to keep the boat vertical no matter which direction the wind was blowing, much to my friend's distress and chagrin they were five hundred miles off course when they arrived at the designated longitude. Hopefully, we will arrive closer to the truth than did those sea adventurers. If that is to be so, we will have to bear with some awkwardness along the way.

A word needs to be said about the sexist language of the manuscript. All of the correspondents for the study were men. I am sure that there are very successful women in pastorates, and that there must be some who fit the criteria for which I looked. Nevertheless, when I attempted to mix the gender of the pronouns throughout the manuscript it created a good deal of awkwardness. Thus I have consistently kept masculine pronouns. Partially to blame is my mother tongue that does not allow personal pronouns in the third person singular without expressing gender.

1

A Composite Profile
of the Successful Pastor

*I have yet to see a dynamic, committed church with a
vibrant lay ministry that is not led and challenged by
the dynamic, committed, vibrant ministry of some pastor who knows that his or her ordained ministry is the
essential sign and focus for the shared ministry of all
Christians within that congregation.*
                         William H. Willimon in
                         Worship As Pastoral Care

Even though success is for many people a much greater
illusion than reality, it would be overly cynical to say that
success is a mirage on the horizon of vanity. There is
authenticity to a job well done. A person has inner satisfaction in the knowledge of having given his or her
best—no matter how platitudinous it may sound to the
philosopher who believes he is above such trivial assessment.

While freely granting the final assessment of life to
God, this book presumes that the pastor whose congregation is experiencing numerical growth must be doing
something right. We stress the word *something*, because
we readily admit that there may be something amiss in
the person who is attracting large numbers of people

seeking spiritual direction. Yet to debunk church growth as an ego trip of an inane enthusiast is to ignore the human potential that is expanded and charged by the Holy Spirit.

It is also possible that the people in today's growing churches would become more mature Christians than they are were they to sit under the ministry of someone else. That we have no way of determining, so we have to begin with what we can evaluate. Unless they *know* something to the contrary, most church leaders presume their successful pastors possess a rightness about who they are and what they are doing. Our curiosity is piqued about what kinds of persons they are, and what they have incorporated into their style and methodology. Much has been written about the characteristics of growing churches, but little close examination has been done of the men who make these churches work in contemporary America. The following pages seek to correct that.

Composite Profile[1]

The typical pastor we interviewed is forty-nine years old, stands five feet eleven inches, and weighs 186 pounds. He is married, with three children. His wife is not employed outside of the home and devotes full time to domestic affairs and the ministry of the church. He has a seminary degree and has been pastor of his present church for thirteen years. His current annual salary is $53,000, which includes housing and all fringe benefits.

Over the last thirteen years his church has enjoyed very rapid numerical growth. When he came to this church, 322 people attended on Sunday morning. It presently averages 1,676 for the morning worship service, with a membership of 1,669. This means that his church has seen over 17 percent annual growth and 270 percent decadal growth during his tenure. The present size of his church places it within the top 1 percent of all churches in America. He was not the founding pastor of the church nor did he serve as an associate on its staff before he became its senior pastor.[2]

Education

Our successful pastor highly values education and ministerial training and has no regret over the extent of his professional education. Several respondents regret having gone to a liberal seminary, and some expressed concern that they had not received more Bible training. Of the thirty seven who were not seminary graduates, sixteen (43 percent) would have liked to finish a seminary degree. The several areas in which the pastors desired to have more expertise were biblical languages, Christian education, counseling, communications, psychology, and business administration. One pastor, who earns $90,000 per year and heads a church of 3,200 upper-middle class individuals, completed a master's degree program in education and business twenty-five years after seminary graduation.

Type A Personality

This composite pastor considers himself to be high key, aggressive, a Type A personality, but not extremely so (Friedman-Rosenman). He moves from task to task rapidly, but in a controlled, thought-out manner. He is time conscious, for he is convinced there is a mission that needs to be accomplished. Time is one of his greatest assets; he must discipline himself to allow a person or event to interrupt his time. He possesses a time urgency undergirded with the grace of patience that allows for unforeseen contingencies. This grace, however, does not allow the pastor fully to escape the tension between being and doing. Ministry walks a fine line between accomplishment and acquiescence.

The pastor's urgency is fueled not so much by a sense of guilt as it is by his overall conception that he is involved in a transcendent business. Working for God can

be quite inspiring. The fifty-five hours a week on the job
do not qualify the pastor as a workaholic but as a person
who is highly committed to the task at hand. To keep
from being consumed by the job, the pastor allows
approximately four hours per week for exercise and five
hours per week for recreation. Such diversions allow him
to attack the rest of the week with renewed vigor accompanied by more acute physical and mental alertness. He
knows that physical exercise is one of the foremost prescriptions against burnout.

What differentiates the highly energized pastor from
the antacid-dependent, Type A, high-tech salesman or
corporate planner is that he has no quota to fill or acquisition of numbers he must demonstrate. Though the pastor of the large church has acquired a comfortable
lifestyle, his acquisitiveness is within the bounds of an
adequate, though not exorbitant, salary ($53,000).
Meeting his monthly mortgage is not predicated on com-
missions generated by a super sales month. Activity is
energized by free choice rather than enslavement or
absorption.

The highly successful pastor, although often feeling
hemmed in by the many demands on his time and personality, will not demonstrate the extreme disorders of a
Type A personality—vocal explosiveness that betrays
aggression and hostility, hurrying the speech of others, or
overwhelming irritation at the slow pace of others. He
may, however, engage in polyphasic thought or performance, that is, doing two or more things simultaneously,
such as dictating a letter while driving the car or planning a church function or solving a problem while exercis-
ing or playing golf.

The supercharged pastor needs to tell himself constantly to slow down rather than hurry up. There never seems
to be enough time. Overbooking is the pastor's greatest
temptation. Time-space limitations repeatedly turn the
illusion of omnipresence into tension and frustration. The
meeting of ever-present deadlines can cause a ministry to

grow shallow and superficial. There is the danger of creative energy being sapped and responses to people becoming mechanized.

Whether the pastor is completely consumed by his Type A personality hinges on whether he sees time and people as gifts from God or means for his own achievement. When numbers of people are goals to be achieved, relationships lose their richness, for the "now" quality of life is replaced by the "not yet" fulfillment of acquisition. There is a similarity between the acquisition of people and the acquisition of money. People become currency units rather than ends in themselves. Accumulation of people within a certain amount of time echoes the boast of the businessman's healthy profit at the end of the year. In the words of Meyer Friedman, "It is the number of dollars, not the dollars themselves that appeases—but unfortunately only partially—the insecurity of the Type A man" (Friedman 1974:74). Such insecurity may furnish a deep unrest for the pastor who on the outside appears to be placid and tranquil. At the base of the insecurity is what Reinhold Niebuhr calls the "sin of seeking security at the expense of other life" (Niebuhr 1964:182).

Type A pastors will have to appropriate grace constantly to fulfill their general insecurities, which are accented by a highly competitive society. The examination of motives is important for all of life, but is doubly important when the life quality and eternal destiny of others is at stake. This is why Jesus made such scathing attacks on the ministry of his own day, a ministry that made stringent demands on the populace for the purpose of enhancing the significance of the demander. The pastor must be aware that achievement provides greater security within the American scheme than aristocracy, inheritance, or even the acquisition of earthly goods. Again, Reinhold Niebuhr is perceptive:

> The truth is that man is tempted by the basic insecurity of human existence to make himself doubly secure and by

the insignificance of his place in the total scheme of life to prove his significance. The will to power is, in short, both a direct form and an indirect instrument of the pride which Christianity regards as sin in its quintessential form (Niebuhr 1964:192).

Such insecurity is fed by the admiration of people, acclamation by superiors, invitations to share success stories with others, and further demands on the pastor's time and resources. Instead of being able to bask in receiving the bishop's award for the year, his "achievements must constantly increase to satiate an appetite that, unchecked by other restraints, ceaselessly increases" (Friedman 1974:75). He must remind himself constantly that his innermost security rests in God's smile of approval rather than the "pace of his status enhancement," a pace that "depends upon a maximal number of achievements accomplished in a minimal amount of time" (Friedman 1974:76–77).

Thus it may be paramount for the pastor not only to take time daily to fellowship with God but also to take two or three days a month geographically removed from the "ministry territory." These extended breaks can be used for basically two things. One is the pastor's need to maintain an objective, long-range view of ministerial values by asking God to scrutinize his priorities, objectives, and motives for ministry. Secondly, extended periods of time need to be spent with spouse and children, so that a checkup can be done on those areas that are most important—relationships and communication with those who are his first order of responsibility. Being in touch with God's creation and immediate family will be aids in cleansing from accumulated hostility, aggression, and guilt that result from unrealistic performance expectations. In being a pastor there is a precarious line that separates ministry to other persons from struggle against other persons. Jesus was highly aware of this line. That is why he often took a boat ride or slipped out into the wilderness.

There is a final distinct difference between the classic Type A personality as described by Meyer Friedman and the subject of our study. The Type A person perceives himself as captain of his fate, master of his soul. True, the successful pastor has a heightened sense of his destiny, but this orientation is of a secondary nature. His primary orientation revolves around God's grace and power and includes a high sense of the contingency of existence. Thus almost three out of four of these men practice fasting: abstinence from food for periods of time for the sake of spiritual power. They literally believe the words of Christ in reference to the casting out of a demon—that this kind of deed can be accomplished only through prayer and fasting (Mark 9:29). The practice of fasting says, "I take spiritual and social responsibility for a situation, but the final outcome is in God's hands. Whatever power and authority I experience proceeds from God's authority and power."

Jungian Personality Types

Over three-fourths of those polled understood themselves to be extroverted.[3] This type pastor has little inhibition in meeting new people and then being at home with them. He is more likely to be the first to greet someone than to be greeted. His natural aptitude would render him very unsatisfied in a vocational world of inanimate objects. Though the pastor is heavily involved with ideas and the increase of his knowledge inventory, his activity is a means to an end: the healing and nurturing of people. He is no philosopher or scientist who is content with sheer contemplation or the observation of data.

The pastor of the numerically growing church is different from the contemplative holy man, and his world is mainly outer rather than inner. None of the surveyed pastors consider themselves to be pious. Piety in today's religious terminology prepares a person for the monastery but not ministry to the outside world. An over-

ly pious posture would remove the pastor from the world
of people and the sheer pragmatism of meeting the exi-
gent crises of day-by-day pastoral life. There is a tension
in choosing between the absolutes of the inner world and
a pastoral methodology that works best for now. But the
pastor's extroversion allows him to roll with the punches
and keep a smile on his face in the crucible of conflict. His
world is more objective than subjective. But herein lies
the danger. In the words of Carl Jung:

> A too extroverted attitude can also become so oblivious of
> the subject that the latter is sacrificed to so-called objec-
> tive demands—to the demands, for instance, of a continu-
> ally expanding business, because orders are piling up and
> profitable opportunities have to be exploited (Jung
> 1971:185).

It is difficult to know whether the pastor is truly extroverted or feels the need to play that role. Whichever it is,
he recognizes that extroversion is crucial to his success.
Friendliness wins more people to the church than meditation, and as Edward Whitmont has pointed out, "Our culture still has a profound distrust of the introvert"
(Whitmont 1969:139). This may be because the introvert
basically mistrusts and fears the outer world of people
and objects. Such a pastor would be a conundrum to his
parishioners. I well remember the wishful response of a
man in a store out in the middle of nowhere. When I
stuck my hand in his, greeting him with a smile and iden-
tifying myself as the pastor of such-and-such a church, he
said, "I wish my pastor would do that." No doubt this
rural inhabitant had a pastor who gravitated toward the
world of ideas rather than the world of people. Such is the
potential danger for the young seminary graduate.

The extroverts tend to perceive themselves as intuitive
rather than rationalistic. Sheer rationalism would seem
to extroverts to render them conventional and uninspired
thinkers, "exact, precise, dry pedantic automatons who
attempt to force everything into rational, intellectual for-

mulation" (Whitmont, 1969:148). Such may do for assembly line production but are unsuitable for production in the Kingdom.

The extroverted-intuitive pastor has a high vision quotient. He is constantly looking for opportunities and ways to fulfill them. This ability is as important to being a successful pastor as is monetary instinct to being a stock market analyst. The ability to anticipate, speculate, initiate, and smell possibilities is inherent in a leader. He leaves the other participants in the committee meeting muttering under their breath, "Why didn't I think of that?" In short, the extrovert-intuitionist is the religious entrepreneur. Whatever he does seems to work. He has a prediliction toward problem solving. He perceives solutions to problems that people don't even know they have.

This pastor would have been highly successful as a corporate planner, stockbroker, businessman, or architect, providing there were someone working with him willing to stand behind the curtains and pick up the debris. One of the great secrets of this style of leadership is being surrounded by support staff, such as administrative assistants, secretaries, and accountants, who are willing to do the detail work. Weisberger has made an insightful historical analysis of Dwight L. Moody in comparing him with the great industrialists of his age:

Chicago and Moody were made for each other. The prairie city was already pulsing with its gathered energies. . . . By the time he had been there five years, he was making a respectable annual five thousand dollars, with fifteen thousand dollars laid away to gather interest. Chicago, which in those years was making the fortunes of the Fields, McCormicks and Armours, to name only a handful, seemed on the way to producing another millionaire in Moody. But Moody was a religious man, too, and the peculiar conditions of church life in brawling Chicago dictated another result (Weisberger 1958:181–82).

There is, however, enough rationalism involved to keep

the modern Dwight L. Moodys from being irresponsible visionaries who make fools of themselves at monthly board meetings because they never perceive limitations, research facts, or do their political homework. These pastors somehow manage simultaneously to keep their feet on the ground and their heads in the clouds.

It is significant that only 6 percent noted that they were introverted-intuitive. It is difficult for such a person to cope with the kind of external world to which he is called. A mystic is able to function within the cloister, but is often rendered ineffective for providing pastoral leadership. The key for the pastor is to be on the same wavelength as the people to whom he ministers. Their worlds are filled with concrete, practical reality: the death of a pet, the frustration of work, the win-loss record of their favorite athletic team. The introverted-intuitive person is simply out of touch with the mundane world. Only by developing the judging, feeling facets of his personality would he be able to identify with others and to organize sufficiently the concrete facts needed to implement their dreams and visions. According to Myers-Briggs, "If . . . their judgement is not developed, they cannot criticize their own inner vision, and they tend to reject all judgments from outside. As a result, they cannot shape their aspirations into effective action. Their ideas will go to waste, and they may be regarded only as visionaries or cranks" (Myers 1985:29).

Management Profile

In terms of an operational management profile, the successful pastor understands himself to be a steady-dominant type with a high degree of inducement and an extremely low degree of compliance.[4] This person is highly competitive and would rather fight an uphill battle than coast downhill. He has readily accepted authority and responsibility, which allows him to be a changer of the status quo. He loves new challenges and does not mind attempting the novel or unusual.

Persons who are overwhelmingly dominant tend to be starters, but will quickly turn to some new task because of frustration and impatience. Not so for our subject, however, because he senses, correctly, that his primary personality management trait is steadiness. He is viewed by others as calm, stable, patient, and dependable. He is likely to stay with a task until completion. It takes a good deal to throw him off course. He admits to ownership of the territory he has been allotted; the church is his, the congregation is his, the parish is his, and the city is his. McManus puts it in terms of secular management:

> Loyalty and belonging are very important to him. He develops strong attachments and usually becomes quite possessive. A company becomes his, the task is his, the office or the piece of equipment is his, the family is his. He builds deep ties and finds it difficult to be separated from the people or organization with whom he has these ties for any extended period (McManus 1978:42).

A person who is high in both dominance and steadiness has what the American Management Association calls the persistent-determined personality. This profile spells determination with a capital *D*. "Carry through," fired by a pragmatic objective and fact-oriented approach, will get the job done. This person works best independently, even though he has enough political sagacity to include others. The persistent-determined person is absorbed in his work and takes great pleasure in looking at a project wrought by ingenuity and competence.

The above type of person is not a lone ranger in his leadership style. In that our composite profile demonstrates a high degree of inducement; the pastor "is sensitive to the fine art of compromise and delegation and will prevent others from perceiving him as blunt, overly direct, overly assertive, cold, self-centered and lacking compassion" (McManus 1978:46). There is enough of the inducement quality in the persistent-determined individual not only to be accomplished himself but to involve many others in his accomplishment. This spells influence. Influence is the ability to allow others to realize their fullest potential. Such is the fine art of leadership, the igniting of dormant potential that lies within others. Hickman and Silva define leadership thus:

> . . . the visionary perspective, gained through an inte-grated sense of history, that permits one to know what will work and what will not work, and the passionate per-sistence to stimulate people to strive toward the peak per-formances that enhance both individual and collective well-being (Hickman and Silva 1987:46).

Inducement is the honey that covers the dominant-steady person. Instead of repelling people he has an entic-ing, attractive personality. He has a positive, optimistic outlook on life, and when presented with a possibility, this pastor's first response is "Why not?" A major strength is his ability to meet others and have a positive impact on them. He is self-confident enough to open him-self up, to be more or less transparent so that people "fre-quently are not only willing to trust him, but even reveal to him some of their more protected secrets" (McManus 1978:40).

Still another factor keeps this dominant personality from going off on a tangent or an ego trip. Three out of four respondents stated that they participated in an accountability group with their peers. They did not indi-cate whether this meant other pastors in their denomina-tion or community or whether this group was composed of trusted leaders within their church. At any rate, the response should be taken to mean that there is a group with whom the pastor can meet on a regular basis and with whom he need not fear to be open and vulnerable. Here is his opportunity to share defeats and victories, dreams and doubts, hope and despair. This is especially important, since leadership can be such a lonely position, even within the intimacies of the pastorate. Even Christ confided in an inner circle of friends.

It is no accident that compliance is the lowest factor on the successful pastor's profile. Others are following him, and not vice versa. The compliant person is much more satisfied working within a controlled situation with someone else calling the shots. He tends to be perfectionistic and thus hesitant to tackle a problem or start a project until he has all of the details worked out. And since all details can never be worked out for any venture beforehand, risk taking and decision making are not high on the compliant person's agenda.

Inherent in leadership is decision making. Decision making often means conflict, confrontation, pro-con polarization, and sometimes bearing the responsibility of failure. The compliant person has an overwhelming need to be thought well of. Thus he will go out of his way to avoid rocking the boat and to avoid negating the approval of others. Because this is the style of leadership in many churches, instead of progress there is preserving and conserving maintenance.

The subject of our investigation operates on the theory that the destiny of the church is in his hands. He may be firmly convinced of monergism and give all credit to sovereign grace, but he also is firmly committed to the biblical teaching that whenever God acts he uses people. Not only does God use people, he uses a key person to carry out his plan, within a particular leader, within a particular community, or among a particular people. The pastor believes he is that person "for such a time as this."

When we asked the pastors who wielded the most power within their churches, 18 percent noted the board, 7 percent the congregation, but 67 percent saw themselves as having the most decision-making power in their churches. Whether they do or not isn't the issue. The greatest portion of these pastors think and act as if the power of destiny *is* in their hands, both for themselves and for the congregations they lead. This self-perception is in keeping with the Myers Briggs extroverted-intuitive type who "may sometimes be more positive and confident than their experience in an area warrants" (Myers 1985:21). If the super pastor were reminded of this tendency, he would probably respond, "The greater sin would be to expect too little of myself rather than too much."

Pastor's Perception of His Congregation

One would anticipate a plethora of answers to the open-ended question, "What do you consider to be the dominant characteristic of your congregation?" The responses can be categorized as stylistic, psychological, spiritual, or socio-economic. The following words were used at least two or more times: ministry, worship, active, evangelistic, joy, multidimensional, biblical, unity, excitement. But one characteristic was cited by fifty-two of the ninety-five respondents (55 percent). This particular characteristic is best described as inclusiveness (though only one person actually used the word), and is represented by a cluster of words: compassion, warmth, acceptance, loving, caring, friendly, tolerant, relational, and transparency.

Whether or not the above be true of the congregation is not important for our investigation. What is important is that this is the way the pastor perceives his people. He has either fostered this general characteristic within his congregation through teaching, preaching, and modeling, or he projects it on them out of his own personality. In other words, he himself has a warm, caring, inclusive personality. It is what Scott Peck calls enlarging ego boundaries by extending "one's self for the purpose of nurturing one's own or another's spiritual growth" (Peck 1978:81). Erik Erikson perceives this kind of inclusiveness in personality as a chief ingredient of the wholeness of a person "who emphasizes a sound, organic, progressive mutuality between diversified functions and parts within an entirety, the boundaries of which are open and fluent" (Erikson 1964:92). The opposite personality is totalistic: "An absolute boundary is emphasized: given a certain arbitrary delineation, nothing that belongs inside must be left outside: nothing that must be outside can be tolerated inside" (Erikson 1964:92).

In short, the above exclusivistic characterization signifies a "we four and no more" mentality. It is true that large churches exist that are highly exclusivistic, ideological, and totalistic in their outlook. These churches either appeal to people with like personalities or sufficiently indoctrinate their children so that they insure their likelihood of staying with that denomination or local church. And if we look closely enough, we will discover that the church that succeeds within that psychological framework is led by a highly charismatic and gifted personality.

The pastor who is able to enhance the attitudes of toleration and openness within his congregation has within himself a strong sense of identity. For whatever reasons, he has been able to negotiate successfully the developmental stages of life. His ability to adapt and high awareness of who he is help him to allow others to be who they are. The church does not tell newcomers there is an immediate standard to which they have to conform.

Ironically, religion has served both to enhance acceptance, toleration, and love and also to intensify bigotry, prejudice, and totalism. The latter attitude has been caused by an early breakdown of trust, a severe disappointment in a world that was supposed to be coherent and faithful. If breakdown occurs too often, the individual exemplifies mistrust of the world and of new encounters with that world. The successful pastor is one who realizes the church has a great opportunity to bridge the mistrust and estrangement that people are experiencing in their everyday world. Millions of people are looking for a warm, loving congregation which is the antidote to alienation. In the words of Erikson:

> Trust, then, becomes the capacity for faith—a vital need for which man must find some institutional confirmation. Religion, it seems, is the oldest and has been the most

lasting institution to serve the ritual restoration of the sense of trust in the form of faith while offering a tangible formula for a sense of evil against which it promises to arm and defend man (Erikson 1968:106).

The above warmth and acceptance does not mean a superficial latitudinarianism, easy believism, or neglect of cardinal Christian beliefs. In fact, there are churches that are psychologically inclusive while remaining doctrinally exclusive. Theological rigidity provides a coherent world, a world that makes sense, founded on absolutes, and defined within limitations. Such was the argument of Dean Kelley in his seminal work, *Why Conservative Churches Are Growing*. Kelley states, "The right thing (in functional terms) for religious organizations to do is to explain life in ultimate terms to their members so that it makes sense" (Kelley 1972:150).

Kelley also recognizes the inherent conflict between warm acceptance and the necessity of asking people for total commitment to an eternal truth. Kelley delineates this paradox with the following statements:

> On the one hand, ultimate meaning is essential to human life, and it is effective to the degree that it demands and secures a central commitment in men's lives. Yet on the other hand, to attain that central significance, it often rides roughshod over other interests and values, sometimes even disregarding human well-being (Kelley 1972:164).

Many pastors proceed with the task in just the terms Kelley has described. They are abrasive in their demeanor and seek to conform converts to a nondeviating and noncompromising standard in whatever manipulative way they believe will best suit their purposes. The practitioner of such a *modus operandi* does not perceive persons as ends in themselves with each having a unique background, a unique set of problems, and a unique course to chart on life's troubled seas.

In short, the inclusive church, or any other organization, needs to put the individual ahead of the organization. In predicting which companies will succeed in the future, Hickman and Silva state, "Organizations must institutionalize principles of moral nobility and act to preserve and maintain conditions that lead to the self-actualization of all stakeholders—employees, investors, customers and competitors" (Hickman and Silva 1987:259).

Pastor's Perception of His Role

The successful pastor senses that he fulfills the pastor (shepherding) role more than any other persona. Fifty-one percent of our respondents saw themselves primarily as pastors as opposed to preachers, administrators, students, and teachers. Eighty-nine percent perceived themselves as pastor-preachers, while only 10 percent perceived themselves as teachers, students, or administrators. This is surprising, especially in the light of the increased administrative tasks in a megachurch. When the pastors were asked to rate the congregations' perceptions of their pastors, pastoral modality was intensified to 60 percent, and the preacher modality was lessened to just a little over one-half of the pastoral (31 percent).

When queried as to whether they would be considered charismatic, faithful, caring, pious, or professional by their people, 46 percent noted caring and 28 percent rated themselves as faithful. Thus, 74 percent believed themselves to be perceived by the congregation as fulfilling a caring- faithful role. The most astonishing result of this question is that only one person said that he was recognized as predominantly pious by his people. This underscores the fact that a word can pass from a highly prized connotation to a negative meaning. Webster defines the word *piety* as "dutifulness in religion; devoutness" (Webster's *NCD,* 1985:890).

The above indicates we live in an age that promotes

familiarity rather than reverence, that values immanence rather than transcendence, and that understands very little of what our Puritan forefathers were all about. The word *pious* smacks, at least for the modern mind, too much of legalism, austerity, and self-righteousness. What would have been the most desired trait for an American pastor two hundred years ago is the least desired trait today. American churchgoers demand morality but not necessarily piety in their leadership.

I have asked several lay persons in these growing large churches what is the secret of their pastor's success or his dominant characteristic. I rarely hear anything that would even faintly resemble sanctity, holiness, piety, or righteousness. Most answers are relational and not particularly religious: "He cares; he is warm; he is sensitive to the needs of others; he knows when I am hurting; he thinks before he speaks; he gets down where the people are."

Identification with others may be the overwhelming ingredient that people look for in a pastor, but that should not surprise us. The appealing pastor is one who can readily size up felt needs. If James Engel is correct, that people only come to God out of felt needs (Engel 1979:117), then hurting individuals will seek out the pastor and congregation who have the keenest ear for those needs, no matter how trivial they may seem to others.

Relationship to Community: Availability and Evangelism

Our composite pastor is a permanent part of the community, partially reflected by the ownership of his own home (82 percent). Both in theory and practice the successful pastor puts down roots in a community. Identification with the community and its surroundings is important both for him and for his family. He is symbolically saying to his congregation, "I am here to make this my permanent home. I am not looking for greener pastures or for a better appointment. I belong to you and you belong to me." An itinerant episcopal system that appoints pastors to parishes for three years or less will not normally work in late twentieth century America.

Identification and relationships are high priorities on the American value scale. If a pastor is perceived as transitory—blowing in, blowing off, and blowing out—he is perceived as part of the problem rather than the solution. The pastor needs to be a symbol of stability to combat the lack of rootedness or transient nature of a highly mobile society. Whether or not the pastor actually spends all of his ministerial life in a community is not as important as his being perceived as "one of us." When a pastor was asked what was the dominant strength of his nineteen years at a church that had grown from one hundred to nine hundred in attendance, he highlighted the "consistency" of his ministry as compared with the "instability" of others.

The above is highly related to the pastor's definition of evangelism. When given the options of defining evangelism in terms of lifestyle, outreach, preaching the gospel, relationships, or verbal witnessing, 64 percent chose lifestyle. One pastor described evangelism as the "totality of life lived in front of others and on behalf of others for the sake of winning them to Christ." He well understands the maxim: "The world doesn't weary of Christ; it wearies of those of us who claim to be like him but aren't."

Being available for people speaks of permanency and stability. The successful pastor senses the need not only of articulating this to his people on Sunday morning, but also of living it out before the congregation. Modeling a lifestyle that says "I am here and I am available whenever you have a need" is more important than exhorting people to make a verbal witness or to be a part of a witnessing team. A visitor at Phillips Brooks's home took note by his watch that the doorbell of the rectory rang every five minutes. Is that the reason Christ exhorted his

disciples to enter a town and stay in one place (Matt.
10:11)? Brooks's biographer states that the famous
preacher "seemed to have become possessed by his own
ideal that the love of God must reach men through a
human being and as such a medium he was giving himself" (Albright 1961: 319).

Availability does not mean that these pastors discount
the importance of verbal personal sharing and witnessing. Over 98 percent of those queried said that they prac-
ticed personal witnessing, and it can be safely assumed
that they encourage their people to do so. During or after
ministering to someone else's needs it is important to be
able to articulate your own faith.

Priority of Tasks

The need to verbally witness does not necessarily
translate into methodical evangelism or "calling." Eighty-
one percent of our pastors gave high priority to study (46
percent) and administration (35 percent), while only 5
percent gave high priority to calling or training others to
do so (house-to-house visitation for the purpose of evangelism). The pastor spends very little time himself in calling
or directly mobilizing others for that purpose. The percentage of pastors who gave high priority to evangelistic
calling and training who were in the first two years at
their present churches were significantly higher but by
no means a majority (24 percent). The percentage of pastors who placed primary importance on evangelistic visitation dropped from 24 percent to 5 percent during the
thirteen-year-stay (average length in survey) in his
church.

Neither does availability mean that the successful pastor will give a high percentage of his time to counseling.
Only 8 percent gave top priority to counseling, while 18
percent gave primary attention to counseling during the
first year. As the congregation grows in number, the counseling load for the senior pastor drops. This may seem

ironic at first glance, but on second thought makes sense. As a congregation grows, the pastor perceives that he is being overwhelmed by counseling. The choice has to be made between doing little or no counseling and counseling the full extent of working hours. Where does one draw the line as to which counseling to accept or which parishioners to reject? How does one take care of the counseling load for fifteen hundred people? Obviously the senior pastor of the large church has chosen to defer all or most of his counseling load to staff members, lay shepherds, or an outside source.

The bottom line is that as the church grows there is a steady increase in the priority a pastor assigns to administration (from 22 percent to 35 percent) and studying (from 30 percent to 46 percent). In other words, almost half of these pastors gave priority to studying above and beyond all other pastoral duties. As a church grows, the senior pastor renders less and less intimate pastoral care and increasingly more "ex cathedra" pronouncements. Such is the finding of Henry Schorr:

> Pastors from smaller churches ranked worship and personal discipleship as more important to effective ministry than did clergy from larger churches. Conversely, ministers from larger parishes believed Bible knowledge and the ability to communicate effectively were more basic to effectiveness in ministry (Schorr 1984:149).

In other words, the counselor becomes a preacher. The organizational structure of one of the churches in our study specifically states:

> In addition to his pastoring role as an elder, the senior minister is primarily to be a teacher of the Word of God—the Bible. . . . To burden the senior minister with other functions (i.e., fund raising, public relations, administration, counselling, visitation, etc.) is to rob him of study time and devotion to the Word, and forces him to function in gift areas other than his own (*Structure of Ministry*:28).

Evidently the pastors in our study do not perceive a conflict between defining themselves primarily as pastors and not actually doing the work of pastoral care defined in traditional ways. Perhaps it can best be summed up as one astute pastor put it, "I consider my most important task as nurturing my staff." (And his is a large, growing ministry.) The above underscores the fact that capable people adapt to needs as they present themselves, doing whatever the role or situation calls for. Srully Blotnick affirms this adaptation process in his book *Ambitious Men.* His several case studies confirm that successful people change, in that different qualities are needed for beginning an enterprise than for continuing it. Leaders do become managers, and entrepreneurs do become administrators. Blotnick writes:

> While there are indeed instances where someone who has started a company is later seen to be clearly lacking the ability and interest to run it now that it is many times its original size, the fact remains that the majority of entrepreneurs make the transition to the role of manager quite well.
>
> One thing that facilitates the transition is that the founder grows older as the firm grows bigger. That allows him to develop a different view of himself and his activities. Headstrong at the start, determined to do things his own way, he typically becomes more compromising and receptive to suggestions once he ages a little and the company is a going concern. "I have to be more open-minded," many told us. "I simply can't do everything myself anymore" (Blotnick 1987:142–43).

With what specialty people does the senior pastor surround himself? First of all, capable secretaries, then persons to do the music, lead the youth, and give direction to the Christian education program, in that order. Close to half (41 percent) of those who listed the staff of their church designated an administrator within the top three positions. Only 16 percent designated someone who worked specifically in evangelism. No doubt the correct conclusion is that all staff members are expected to participate in evangelistic outreach to some extent. The same would possibly be true of counseling, since only six pastors listed a counselor in their top three positions.

It is evident from the responses that we are an age-conscious church. Workers were listed for every age group: children, junior high, senior high, college, adults, and seniors. Beyond these designations the only thing that can be determined is that churches hire people to fill a plethora of needs: recreation, bookkeeping, custodians, discipling, pastoral visitation, missions, and ethnic ministries. There is no end to the ability of creative pastors to perceive opportunities and suggest to their people that here is a need which should be met by a staff person.

Conclusion

The above is a composite personality description of a pastor of a growing megachurch. None of our pastors perfectly fit that picture. However, this personality probably more closely fits the pastor who produces numerical growth than the contrasting personality who is a compliant, Type B introvert. We do not contend that a ministerial board can choose with certainty a personality type that will produce evangelistic results. God's thoughts are often not our thoughts and his ways are not our ways. Simple cause-and-effect analysis borders on the futile wisdom of humanity. The effective pastor does not automatically fall within a specific personality type.

What this chapter does contend is that there is a high degree of relationship between the personality of a church and its ability to attract people, and the catalyst in that relationship is the psyche of the pastor. I define the effective pastoral psyche as an inner direction enabled by innate or acquired personality traits, which are aggressively applied to the task at hand. Such is God's gift to a congregation for "such a time as this."

Successful Pastor Inventory

1. Name: _____ 2. Age:_____
   (If you wish to remain anonymous, please do so.)
3. What is your: Height _____ Weight _____
4. Married? ☐ Yes ☐ No   5. Children:_____ Ages:_____
6. Denomination: _____
7. Spouse employed full time? ☐ Yes ☐ No
   By the church? ☐ Yes ☐ No Outside the church? ☐ Yes ☐ No
8. Education: Check all that applies to you.

   ☐ High school   ☐ Liberal arts college   ☐ Trade school
   ☐ Bible school   ☐ Seminary   ☐ Other
9. Educationally what would you do differently, if you did it over again (one
   sentence or phrase)?

   _____
10. How long have you been pastor of this church? _____
11. What is your annual gross salary, including social security, insurance,
    pension, housing allowance, etc. (if a parsonage is provided, include the
    rental value)? _____
12. Morning worship attendance: _____
    Sunday evening attendance: _____ Midweek attendance _____
13. Membership: _____
14. Over the last five years your church has increased in attendance by what
    percentage? _____ Over the last ten years? _____
15. How many were in attendance at morning worship when you came to
    this church? _____
16. Did you serve as an associate or on the staff of this church before you
    became the senior pastor? ☐ Yes ☐ No How long? _____
17. Are you the founding pastor? ☐ Yes ☐ No
18. Number of paid church staff full and part time (including secretarial and
    janitorial). _____
    List the positions which are paid full time: 1. _____
    2. _____   3. _____   4. _____
    5. _____   6. _____   7. _____
    8. _____   9. _____   10. _____
19. Choose one: ☐ Own my own home
    ☐ Home church owned   ☐ Rent
20. Which of the following personality types do you feel best describes you?
    ☐ Extroverted-rationalistic   ☐ Introverted-rationalistic
    ☐ Extroverted-intuitive   ☐ Introverted-intuitive
21. According to the Friedman-Rosenman personality analysis, would you
    consider yourself to be a:
    ☐ Type A personality (high-key, aggressive)
    ☐ Type B personality (low-key, laid-back)

22. Which of the following best describes your leadership style?
    □ Dominant □ Steady
    □ Inducive □ Compliant

23. Who has the most power in respect to decision making in your church?
    □ The pastor □ Someone outside of your church (bishop,
    □ The board district superintendent, etc.)
    □ The congregation

24. I would define my ministry as: □ priestly □ prophetical

25. I believe that conversion is:
    □ instantaneous □ indefinite
    □ gradual □ relative

26. We have a regularly scheduled revival at least once a
    year. □ Yes □ No

27. Are you in some type of accountability group with
    your peers? □ Yes □ No

28. Do you practice personal witnessing? □ Yes □ No

29. Do you practice fasting? □ Yes □ No
    If yes, how often?_____

30. During the early growth years of our church, the
    leadership set definite numerical goals. □ True □ False

31. I believe the pastor should be outspoken on social
    issues such as abortion, pornography, etc. □ True □ False

32. I believe the pastor should be outspoken on
    international issues such as *contra* aid, nuclear
    buildup, human rights, etc. □ True □ False

33. I consider my outstanding spiritual gift to be _____ .

34. Assuming that the Holy Spirit is the cause for the success of our church,
    in one sentence, what practical reason would I give for our progress?_
    _____ .

35. In terms of professional ministry I get the most fulfillment out of:____
    _____ .

36. How many hours a week do you give to the pastorate? _____

37. How many nights a week do you have an engagement away from home?
    _____

38. I spend _____ hours a week in recreation.

39. I spend _____ hours a week in physical exercise.

40. Community involvement: How many hours a month do you average
    giving to a service organization (Kiwanis, Jaycees, etc.)? _____

41. On Sunday mornings I preach
    approximately (choose one): On Sunday evenings:
    □ 15 minutes □ 15 minutes
    □ 20 minutes □ 20 minutes
    □ 25 minutes □ 25 minutes
    □ 30 minutes □ 30 minutes
    □ Other □ Other

42. What do you consider to be the dominant characteristic of your congregation? _____

_____

43. What was the topic of the last series of messages which you preached?

_____

44. I spend _____ hours a week in sermon preparation.

45. How much time do you spend alone in prayer with God daily? _____

46. How many chapters of the Bible do you read weekly? _____

47. I spend _____ hours a week reading other than the Bible.

Rank the following questions from most to least. For example, in a question with five choices rank them from 1 (most) to 4 or 5 (least).

48. I perceive myself as a/an:
____ Administrator
____ Pastor
____ Preacher
____ Student
____ Teacher

49. My people perceive me as a/an:
____ Administrator
____ Pastor
____ Preacher
____ Student
____ Teacher

50. My people perceive me mostly as:
____ Charismatic
____ Faithful
____ Caring
____ Pious
____ Professional

51. I would define evangelism as:
____ Lifestyle
____ Outreach
____ Preaching the Gospel
____ Relationships
____ Verbal witnessing

52. Most of the conversions in our church have taken place in the context of:
____ The home
____ Regular church services
____ Evangelistic crusades outside of the church
____ Specially scheduled events, such as a revival

53. Time spent during the past year:
____ Administration
____ Calling on or training others to call on new prospects
____ Calling on people who are already members of the church
____ Counseling
____ Studying

54. Time spent during the first two years of this pastorate:
____ Administration
____ Calling on or training others to call on new prospects
____ Calling on people who are already members of the church
____ Counseling
____ Studying

55. People in America today generally need to be told that they:
____ are loved
____ are sinners
____ are important
____ are good
____ are called

56. Eschatological topics of your preaching:
____ Rapture
____ Heaven and hell
____ God our judge
____ Future as an extension of this life
____ God's kingdom now

57. How do the following terms describe your preaching style (most to least):
____ Doctrinal
____ Evangelistic
____ Exegetical
____ Inspirational

58. The main causes of the problems of most people:
____ Heredity
____ Environment
____ Sin
____ Individual choice

59. If your denomination has a theological distinctive, indicate the emphasis it receives in your preaching and teaching:
    ____ Extremely high
    ____ High
    ____ Moderate
    ____ Low
    ____ Extremely low

60. Define pastoral success in one sentence. _____
    _____
    _____
    _____
    _____

2

Defining Success for the Contemporary Pastor

If there is anyone in the world I pity, it is the one who has no love for his job. I would rather preach than anything else. I have never missed a chance to preach. I would rather preach than eat my dinner or have a holiday, or anything else the world can offer. I would rather pay to preach, than be paid not to preach. It has a price in agony of sweat, tears, and no calling has such joys and heartbreaks, but it is a calling an archangel might covet; and I thank God that of His grace He called me into this ministry. I wish I had been a better minister, but there is nothing in God's world or worlds I would rather be.

Samuel Chadwick

Spiritual pursuit is high on the successful pastors' list of priorities. While piety is a negative for ministerial parameters, spirituality is a must for accomplishing the ministerial task. These words would have once meant the same thing, but today the former connotes religious posturing whereas the latter suggests inward reality.

Being called by God is the first prerequisite for ministerial leadership. Being directed by God on a daily basis is the second. The only way to sense God's direction is to spend time alone with him. Our surveyed pastors spend a daily average of fifty-two minutes in prayer. Only 18 percent fell below a half hour, and almost half (48 percent) spend an hour or more in prayer each day. There is no doubt that the pastor attributes much of his success to the power of God in answer to prayer.

Something else happens when the pastor prays. His sensitivity to others is heightened. Prayer focuses on a Christ who died for all and a Christ who identifies with the deepest hurts that individuals experience. Hebrews 4:15 tells us that "we do not have a high priest who is unable to sympathize with our weaknesses, but we have one who has been tempted in every way, just as we are—yet was without sin." The true priest is touched with the infirmities of others; he walks in their shoes, sees situations from their vantage point, and carries their burdens. This kind of spiritual sensitivity prevents a judgmental or overly condemning spirit. A true shepherd is not overly harsh: "A bruised reed he will not break, and a smoldering wick he will not snuff out" (Isa. 42:3).

The above verse further states, "In faithfulness he will bring forth justice." Christ delicately combined the prophetic and priestly roles. It should not be surprising that an equal number of pastors in our survey designated themselves as either prophets or priests (37 percent each). Twelve percent perceived themselves as both prophet and priest (an answer that was not given as an option). Thus our composite pastor both preaches the word in a forthright manner and makes consolation and understanding a part of that proclamation. He speaks to the people and for the people. He represents God to his flock and represents his flock before God.

Biblical Love

The tension between clinging to orthodox Christian tenets and exhibiting warm nurture is demonstrated in the answers to two survey questions. When the pastors were asked what are the causes of people's problems, 69 percent answered sin, 25 percent individual choice, and 2 percent environment. None gave heredity as a possible cause for people's problems. But when asked whether people need to be told that they are loved, sinners, important, good, or called, 80 percent answered that people need to be told they are loved. In other words, people can be loved without being given a stamp of "okayness." "I can affirm my love for you and God's love for you without affirming that everything is okay between you and God, you and your neighbor, and you and yourself."

The desire for a healthy balance between upholding biblical standards and maintaining a low threshold at the church entrance was articulated in these definitions of success: "a strong Bible emphasis supported by a philosophy of love, acceptance, and forgiveness"; "accepting people where they are—expressing love to them with scriptural personal conviction without condemnation of them"; "the ability to present biblical truth in a positive and relevant way so that it is good news to the individuals to whom you are speaking."

The Primacy of Preaching

The successful pastor is able to reduce the paradox or tension of calling unique people to an absolute standard. He renders unconditional, positive regard to people who, at least for now, have deviated far from the standard he believes God desires for potential converts. One of his chief means is preaching. The importance of preaching has not diminished in the American evangelical pulpit. Today's successful pastor stands squarely within the American Protestant and Puritan tradition. This finding is not unique, in that it was borne out by Samuel Blizzard's 1955 study of 1,111 Protestant parish ministers. Preaching ranked first when a combination of importance, satisfaction, and effectiveness were taken into consideration (Blizzard 1985:5).

When we asked our pastors in an open-ended question from what they receive the most fulfillment in their professional ministry, preaching appeared 57 percent of the time against a multitude of other answers—teaching, discipling, equipping, meeting needs, relationships, counseling, evangelism, and writing. Maturing people in their Christian faith was the next most-mentioned concept—theologically referred to as sanctification—but mentioned in only 11 percent of the returns.

No other ministerial activity rivals the preaching of the successful American evangelical pastor. Thus it has been in American Protestant ministry from its very inception. Our Puritan forefathers dropped much of the sacerdotalism of their Anglican ancestors and made the pulpit central to both pastoral care and worship. Winthrop Hudson traces the "unanimity of emphasis upon the importance of preaching" among the Puritan preachers (Hudson 1956:186). This unanimity was even more solidified within the American conception of pastoral ministry two hundred years later. Few Protestants of any stripe would have differed with the following statement in the *American National Preacher* in 1829:

> While the church is considered as the pillar and ground of the truth, preaching must, beyond all question, be regarded as its most important duty. . . . The preaching of the gospel by the living voice . . . has in all ages been the principle instrument in the hand of God by which the church has been sustained and advanced (Mead 1956:244).

The Content and Style of Preaching

Whether or not the above was true, American preachers believed it, and that is the conviction of successful pastors today. However, preaching has experienced some dramatic shifts over the last one hundred years. The sermon is shorter, more positive in outlook, and less oriented toward conversion or immediate results. It is pragmatic, but its pragmatism is of a different nature than in the past. It is a twentieth-century pragmatism that seeks to instill principles that can be incorporated into everyday living. "Can it be applied to the needs of contemporary persons?" is the ultimate evaluative question.

Sidney Mead has traced the change from the didactic-expository style of the Puritan divines to the conversion-oriented preaching of the nineteenth century evangelists. The storytelling style that displaced careful exegesis was immanently practical and geared to the individual who was standing at the crossroads of hell and heaven. Robert Baird wrote in 1839 that American preaching was designed primarily "to bring men to a decision and to make them decide right on the subject of religion" (Mead 1956:245).

While the practicality of preaching has been retained, the call for immediate decision making as it relates to conversion or some other milestone experience on the order of salvation has diminished. Almost four out of five of our queried individuals stated that they believed conversion to be instantaneous as opposed to gradual, indefinite, or relative (9 percent saw it as a combination of gradual and instantaneous). Where do these conversions take place? Fifty-four percent of the respondents said in regular church services, and a full 93 percent said in the home or regular church services as opposed to specially scheduled revivals or evangelistic crusades. This statistic is surprising in view of the fact that almost seven out of ten of these pastors still have regularly scheduled revival campaigns with their churches.

Even though conversion is considered to be instantaneous, it takes place in the context of preaching that is nurturing, equipping, and maturation oriented. In the list of topics of our pastors' most recent series of messages the words *prayer* and *family* were most often used—eleven times between them. Other topics included discipline, faith, stewardship, commitment, missions, outreach, and personal witnessing. Many of the titles revealed their pragmatic slant: "The Winning Spirit," "How to Experience Spiritual Renewal," "Building the Walls of Your Life," "What to Do with Your Sins," "Authority of the Believer," "Back to Basics," "Making Christ at Home." Other titles indicated the contemporary thrust of preaching: "Issues of the Eighties," "Bible Answers to Most-Often Asked Questions."

The respondents were almost equally divided between topical (46 percent) and expository (44 percent) preaching. A sermon series was designated expository if a portion of Scripture was listed (Book of John, Romans, etc.) without a topic. (Those who listed portions of Scripture may have been preaching with a particular issue in mind.) Haddon Robinson would designate this kind of preaching *topical exposition* (Robinson 1980:56).

There is a direct correlation between expository preaching and education. The higher a preacher has progressed in professional training, the more expository he perceives himself to be. Twenty percent of those who had only a Bible school education perceived themselves as exegetical, as compared with 41 percent of liberal arts graduates and 56 percent of seminary graduates. Six percent of the total designated their preaching as doctrinal, 16 percent evangelistic, 46 percent exegetical, and 29 percent inspirational, while 9 percent actually listed doctrinal themes on which they had preached: Holy Spirit, holiness, Lamb of God, the second coming.

Doctrine and Preaching

On the whole, American evangelical preachers who attract people are not doctrinally oriented, at least not in their preaching. Protecting or conserving doctrine is secondary to their offering practical biblical truths that can be implemented now in the listener's life. This contemporary preaching principle is evidenced by such sermon titles as "Investments, People, Things" and "Handles for Holy Living." Very few of the preachers would receive awards for being "overt defenders of the faith."

Church members are much less likely to hear doctrinal messages on the key subjects that are at the heart of evangelical theology, such as justification by faith or original sin, than they are to hear messages on "felt-need" topics such as marriage, family, and other crisis areas. James Engel argues that people are less likely to listen to abstract principles than they are to communication that starts where they live. However, ministry to felt need, according to some, "can be quite superficial and completely overlook the true dimensions underlying a person's situation at any given point in time" (Engel 1979:117).

There is the danger of today's preaching becoming teleological or utilitarian to the point of centering on the individual. Some would criticize the following title, actually preached by one of our subjects, as being too anthropological or self-oriented: "How the Holy Spirit Can Help You Have Super Achievements in Your Life." Preaching today has to do with the practical issues of here and now rather than the eschatological issues of forever and ever. Peter Berger's allegation, although written in 1969, would still prove true:

It is safe to say that, compared to earlier historical periods, fewer Americans today adhere to the churches out of a burning desire for salvation from sin and hellfire, while many do so out of a desire to provide moral instruction for their children and direction for their family life, or just because it is part of the life style of their particular neighborhood (Berger 1969:5).

On the other hand, we must not assume that the pastor of the successful growing church completely camouflages his theological or doctrinal profile. The responses to "If your denomination has a theological distinctive, indicate the emphasis it receives in your preaching and teaching" created an almost perfect bell curve, with only 25 percent giving it extremely high or extremely low emphasis. Overall, it did not appear on the survey that there are conscious or concentrated efforts on the parts of the preachers to minimize doctrine to attract people, only that no sermon title indicated that the pastors are heavily involved in explicating what their churches or denominations believe, particularly not during the worship services.

Several pastors expressed the philosophy that they will remove, as much as is possible, theological jargon, or doctrinaire and religious clichés, from their Sunday morning preaching. One such is Bill Hybels at Willow Creek Community Church in South Barrington, Illinois. It is Hybels's belief that the services on Sunday morning (and Saturday night) should be "Christianity 101," so that the entry point for nonbelievers can be as wide as possible.

Preaching and Unconditional Positive Regard

When the pastors indicated the topic on which they preached in their last series, they included nothing controversial, negative, condemning, or bent toward eternal damnation. Preaching is one of the chief means by which pastors exhibit their unconditional positive regard of their listeners. They are convinced that preaching needs to be a balm to those seeking solace. (The question arises whether one can be true to the mandate of God's Word and the attributes of his character and still be as enticing from the pulpit as some pastors are. This will be addressed later.)

Others believe that the delicate balance between accepting people as they are and calling them to repentance can be maintained. Thomas Oden addresses this very question, arguing that only through loving people can an individual value himself anew, and only by renewed self-value can he value others and be freed "from the self-righteous anxiety, guilt, and defensiveness that prevent him from loving his neighbor" (Oden 1966:74). Oden does not argue for a love that disregards the seeker's guilt and responsibility for grace and repentance. Facing the reality of guilt is important for the therapeutic process, because it allows a person to confess it and to make acts of restitution where possible. Persons who are free to express their guilt and negated values instead of simply covering up their acts have fewer symptoms of pathological disorder. Oden writes, "The only real cure to be found is in acts of actual restoration, which change the objective situation so that one no longer feels guilty and needs to hide it" (Oden 1974:95).

The general description of today's preaching by today's successful pastors is that it is positive, upbeat, practical, biblical, nonconfrontational, and brief. Yes, brief compared with the standards of yesteryear when God had little competition and George Whitefield held thousands spellbound for nine hours at a time with only short intermissions. The mean preaching time for contemporary preachers is thirty minutes Sunday morning and thirty-four minutes Sunday evening. Only one person indicated an hour in the morning and two people an hour or more in the evening.

Neither do pastors exert energy and conserve time during the week as did Jonathan Edwards and Increase Mather in their ten-to-twelve-hour days in the study. The latter, according to Harry Stout, "took the emphasis on preaching to an extreme even by colonial standards, immersed himself in his study and invariably regretted 'time lost by visitants' who came to see him apart from his posted hours" (Stout 1986:91). But neither do today's successful pastors have anything to be ashamed of, as they weekly average seventeen hours in sermon preparation and read twenty chapters in the Scriptures. Within the fifty-five-hour workweek, which was the average indicated, our respondents gave over one-quarter of their time to sermon preparation. The preaching task is taken seriously by successful pastors.

Noncontroversial Pulpit

The kinds of issues in which the pastor involves himself indicate the noncontroversial manner of his preaching and teaching. Eighty-nine percent said that the pastor should be outspoken on social issues such as abortion and pornography. But when asked if the pastor should be outspoken on international issues such as *contra* aid, nuclear weapons buildup, or human rights, 60 percent responded negatively. These men tend to work under the philosophy that they should address only issues that have a clear or self-evident moral tone to them: alcoholism, obscenity, marital fidelity. They believe these issues are more easily addressed from the biblical perspective (Judeo-Christian Decalogue) and are part of the traditional evangelical moral code, especially those areas having to do with sexual purity.

Issues with multiple nuances, that are not so easily addressed from the Bible, and have political overtones are not considered by many of the pastors to be within their prerogative. If such issues as nuclear weapons buildup are important, they are only of secondary importance. Of primary importance is preaching the gospel. The pastor reasons, "Why should I negate someone coming to Christ by stepping out on an issue about which I may have feelings, but for which I do not have clearcut biblical answers? If I cannot precede it with a 'Thus saith the Lord,' then perhaps I had better express my opinion in private rather than release it in public." Has today's successful pastor been too conservative in his remarks, as the following statement from Harold Bosley might suggest?

> Silence may be golden, as the proverb has it, for most men most of the time, but not so for the preacher confronted by the unfolded issues of the life of his time. . . . If he belongs to the great tradition of preaching, he will know that it is better to be wrong than be silent in the face of the problems that are tormenting the thought and lives of his people (Bosley 1969:33).

The "Nowness" of Preaching

Probably the most critical difference between preaching today and preaching of even twenty-five years ago is the immediacy of preaching. Preaching is in the now. It has little to say about the past and even less to say about the future. Ozora S. Davis correctly says: "In spite of the common charge against preaching that it is bound to doctrine and tradition, there is no area of thought and action that is more quickly responsive to the influence of the age than the Christian pulpit" (Quoted by Sager 1969:260). This is the Pepsi generation, the generation that sacrifices little for the future and nothing for eternity. The prophetical warnings of our Puritan forefathers, or the "get ready for the rapture or else" of twentieth-century fundamentalism are hardly to be found within the homilies of popular ministers.

When the pastors of our survey rated the eschatological emphasis of their preaching, 51 percent emphasized God's kingdom now, 14 percent stressed the future as an extension of this life, 13 percent gave attention to God as our judge, 11 percent gave first priority to the rapture and a mere 5 percent attached primary importance to heaven and hell. In other words, almost twice as many of these pastors emphasized nontraditional understandings of eschatology as did traditional understandings. The growing congregation assumes that appealing to the here-and-now needs of persons will be more effective in producing spiritual maturity than focusing on the rewards of heaven or the fears of hell. Such reasoning can be debated, of course, as the following by Malcolm Muggeridge suggests: "The only ultimate disaster that can befall us, I have come to realize, is to feel ourselves to be at home on earth" (Muggeridge 1969:48). But for now, the preachers are preaching to middle-class listeners who are very comfortable on this planet and not likely to sing "This World Is Not My Home."

Service Organizations

Seventy percent of the queried pastors give no time

whatsoever to service organizations such as Kiwanis and Jaycees. Only 10 percent give five hours or more per week. Such limited participation in community social groups is a critical indicator of the large-church pastor's mentality. First of all, he is sold on the church as God's instrument to effect change within our society. If the local church is doing all that needs to be done in a community, there is little or no need for his involvement in other social organizations. One of the main functions of the church is to provide service opportunities. If these are properly taken advantage of by the church's constituents, they, too, have no need for seeking other opportunities.

But there is a bias that is even more critical. While other organizations may do some good, they do not couple their efforts with a presentation of the gospel. The pastor believes that a social-change effort that represents Christ is far more effective than one that doesn't. It is better to give one's time and energy to a kingdom enterprise than to a secular one. Kingdom enterprises are best defined from the pulpit and not by service organizations.

Defining Success

No two pastors defined success exactly the same. Many of the answers made paramount their own relationships with God: "loving God"; "doing the will of God"; "hearing God rather than man"; "obedience to the call"; "to be what God wants me to be"; "pleasing God"; "obeying the voice of God"; "submission to Christ"; "faithfulness to God's call"; "sensitivity to God's leadership"; "being a man of God, right with God."

A large percentage of the definitions indicated that "being" a certain type of person was of utmost importance to success: "being in the place where Christ is building his church"; "being the best person you can be to the glory of God"; "pastor exemplifying total commitment"; "the life of a man in love with Christ lived before others"; "the certainty of Christ in one's life, and yieldedness to the authority of the Bible"; "discipleship lifestyle"; "right place at right time with right message and accompanying gifts and graces"; "trying to be God's man for the hour."

Almost two-thirds of the respondents defined success as "bringing about a particular effect within the lives of those to whom they are ministering through loving, leading, equipping, discipling, maturing, winning, reaching, protecting, teaching, training, building, sending, and ministering." Success in ministry for most of these men is doing something with a definite end result or product in mind. Much of the goal orientation had a theocentric thrust: "helping people to find full life in Christ"; "the progressive achievement of God's goals in God's people in God's time"; "build a great church for God"; "winning and maturing people in Christ"; "making disciples by teaching all the things that Jesus taught"; "seeing people grow to be all that God has planned for them"; "leading a group of people positively as thinking individuals in Christ through a very negative and personally dangerous world"; "enabling people to choose freely wholeness in Jesus Christ and with one another so they are maturing to make disciples of all people."

Other definitions of pastoral success were much more anthropological and teleological. Doing was not an end in itself, but was for the purpose of bringing desired results either in the church or in the lives of individuals. Theocentric and christological orientations were either absent or simply presumed: "loving watch-care over the church and creating an atmosphere of love, acceptance, and excitement to the level where others want to be a part of it"; "motivate others to do what they don't want to do and enjoy doing it"; "meeting the needs of your people under all their varying pressures, failures, and successes"; "observing people mature to the point where they reach people"; "maturing the flock to reproduce"; "equipping and making people successful"; "meeting people's needs by whatever method it takes"; "dream dreams— find needs—love people."

Many definitions of success indicated the pastor's concern with not only living a productive life but also demonstrating a lifestyle that was consistent with his message, thereby confirming his intrinsic experience by his extrinsic action. One pastor wrote, "Delicate balance between presenting the gospel effectively and living the gospel consistently." Others wrote: "the certainty of Christ in one's life and yieldedness to the authority of the Bible"; "leaving behind an example that he was kind and faithful"; "the life of a man in love with Christ lived before others"; "equipping my people by example and by precept to build up the body of Christ in love"; "model Christ attractively"; "pastor exemplifying total commitment." It was important for these men to model Christianity as they interpreted it and to be able to say, "I practice what I preach. My greatest sermon is my life. I want to grow with my people into the kind of local church God has in mind for the community."

The quotations in the above paragraph again are in keeping with Blizzard's study:

> Character was mentioned most frequently as a personality characteristic of the effective parish minister. This was seen as involving inner direction. Specifically, this category included such characteristics as purity, sincerity, sense of responsibility, and trustworthiness (Blizzard 1985:46).

The effective pastor has confidence in the congruence between his inner qualities and outward demands. He is convinced that disjuncture here will lead to ultimate defeat.

A few pastors indicated that they view dependency on the Holy Spirit while they are doing the task as being as important as the results of the task. One pastor defined success as "ministering to the needs of people with the love of Jesus Christ and in the power of the Holy Spirit." Other definitions included: "fruitfulness because of being right with God and close to Christ"; "being an instrument of God." No success definition more clearly expressed human dependency on the Divine than the following: "giving one's lunch to Jesus and watching him feed a crowd with it."

Not one definition indicated that success is predicated on numbers. Many definitions indicated that success could be much better measured by qualitative rather than quantitative results. Whether or not quality can be measured, there is greater validity in producing particular characteristics in people than in simply adding people to church rolls. These pastors are convinced that the church needs something more than more Christians; what the church needs is more Christians who are more Christian than they already are. Such Christians are the church's gift to the world.

Although eschatology may have been implicit in several of the definitions, only two of the pastors made it explicit. One wrote, "Well done, thou good and faithful servant," and the other, "Getting people home." The median age of these two men is sixty; perhaps success is more succinctly crystalized as one stands on Mt. Pisgah. Accomplishment has a more futuristic nuance at the end of one's vocational trek than at the beginning.

Conclusion

The overall impression is that the successful pastor believes his ministry to be spiritually oriented rather than intellectually, educationally, or technically determined. Study without prayer is futile. Study with prayer produces preaching that, at least in the perception of the preacher, represents the mind of God. The shepherd expects the sheep to follow, because he has received directions from the Lord. He believes himself to be a "spiritual" man, for "the natural man cannot hear the voice of God, neither can he know it, because it is spiritually discerned" (see 1 Cor. 2:14).

Hearing the voice of God the preacher renders the pulpit a place of affirmation and proclamation rather than compromise and debate. Convictions are more important than dialectics. Having conviction means that the pastor will teach his people to believe their beliefs and doubt their doubts, rather than doubt their beliefs and believe their doubts. His proclamation provides the authority that millions of Americans are seeking in their search for life's answers. Such a pastor knows where he is going and does not hesitate to invite "whosoever will" to follow. A pillar of fire by night and a cloud by day are worth far more than the latest theology or philosophy. His people expect him to preface life's prescriptions with "Hear the word of the Lord."

Therefore, the pastor believes his supreme task is leadership mediated through prayer and preaching. Prayer without preaching produces a monastic, and preaching without prayer produces a monologue. Wisdom from above enables the pastor to lead his people through dialogue, sensing where people are and where they need to go. His proclamation is authentic because he understands human nature and the possibilities of grace. His inner direction proclaims outer conviction for forward motion. There have always been and always will be innumerable multitudes willing to follow gladly those who are certain of where they are going. Leading people in the right direction spells success.

3

The Successful Pastor's Personal Qualities

"Whatever your hand finds to do, do it with all your might" (Eccles. 9:10a).

Success is the child of confidence and perseverance. The talent of success is simply doing what you can do well, and doing well whatever you do—without a thought of fame. Fame never comes because it is craved. Success is the best test of capacity. Success is not always a proper criterion for judging a man's character. It is certain that success naturally confirms us in a favorable opinion of ourselves. Success in life consists in the proper and harmonious development of those faculties which God has given us.

The Royal Path of Life, 1876

An attempt to distill the criteria of successful ministry into its basic elements would be futile. It could also be arbitrary and opinionated, because after all, what we received from the questionnaires was subjective interpretation and not quantifiable data we could verify. The trajectory of ministry cannot be forecast with the same accuracy as a computerized moonshot. No matter how scientifically accurate and even biblically and theologically sound it may be, a prediction of success or failure is bludgeoned by the many exceptions to the rule.

59

Martin Wells Knapp, who founded God's Bible School in Cincinnati, is a case in point. A. M. Hills, Knapp's biographer, said that his subject looked as if he had been thrown together by some laughable accident of nature. The first impression that he made was almost always unfavorable. When he went to preach his first trial message, he overheard someone in the background say, "Well, what did you bring him here for?" Knapp, who stood five feet four inches and weighed 120 pounds, was sick and physically emaciated most of his life. But Knapp defied the odds by seeing thousands converted under his ministry, writing nine books, establishing a Bible school in the early twentieth century that is presently enjoying some of its best days, establishing a mission in Africa, and publishing a periodical with fifty thousand subscribers. Along with Seth Rees, father of Paul Rees, he was cofounder of a denomination, the Pilgrim Holiness Church.

Three things shape a person's destiny: heredity, environment, and unique experience. Most of us can do very little about the first two, especially during our early years of life. In fact, it may be debatable what can be done about the third, but there is no doubt that Knapp had a unique experience. He was filled with the Holy Spirit. Knapp often testified to the infilling of the Holy Spirit and recorded in his journal such phrases as "He comes and fills me anew." A. M. Hills said this of his subject: "Brother Knapp was one of these divine surprises. . . . I consider Brother Knapp the greatest surprise, the most truly Spirit-filled, Spirit-guided, Spirit-illuminated, and Spirit-empowered man I have known. There was in him relatively the least of the human and the most of the Divine" (Hills 1973:18, 420).

Most evangelical leaders would say amen to the above, but that does not keep district superintendents, bishops, and seminary professors from pulling their hair out over the dismal failures of those they have trained and sent into the ministry. Not only were sincere efforts made to equip these men, but the necessity of depending on the Holy Spirit was urgently preached to and instilled in them. The desperation of leadership to rejuvenate dying churches and quicken lethargic pastors is demonstrated by the multiplication of self-helps for pastors and quick-fix seminars. The array of opportunities and methods that will "turn one's ministry around" is perplexing, and sometimes downright deceptive—whether or not it is meant to be. This is not to say that attempts at reviving ministry are not honest and intentions are not pure, but quite often they fail.

Four years ago a conference of approximately sixty churches hired one of the top exponents of church growth in the country to speak to them on the principles of evangelism and leadership. Some believe this man to be one of the top motivational speakers in the country. I personally know him to be a dynamic communicator and powerful persuader. He is a salesman *par excellence*. I was responsible for giving many of the seminar participants seminary credit for this experience. In the written critiques of the sessions I required, the presenter and the presentation drew raving reviews. Some of my students thought it to be the greatest learning experience of their lives. In fact, in approximately twenty responses only one student ventured to say anything negative at all. He tacitly suggested that the speaker may be spending too much time at the church and not enough time with his family, and his priorities may need to be restructured.

What, then, was the ministerial track record over the next four years of those thirty-eight pastors who participated in the seminar? Thirteen of the pastors moved. Five of them dropped out of ministry completely because of retirement, frustration, or whatever. Of the twenty remaining, twelve experienced no numerical growth or even declined in their churches. Among the eight pastors whose churches did grow, only one had a decadal growth rate of over 100 percent in morning worship attendance, which church-growth analysts assess as excellent.

Would the above results be far removed from the progress of many pastors and churches that have employed such a method to give them a shot in the arm? The speaker promised that what he had to give them "would change their lives." But what I tell students and others preparing for ministry is that it is entirely unlikely that one seminar, one class, or one method will radically change their lives or ministry. He who would do good must do it in minuscule particulars, and he who would proceed must do so in minute increments.

Expectations of one giant step forward are often illusory. In fact, they are often self-defeating. One of the reasons is that principles for success normally come from highly successful people. These people are not successful because of their principles; the principles are results of their success and their highly motivated personalities. Separated from the special personality the principles do not work. I would not negate the possibility of picking up some good ideas at a relevant, well-conducted seminar, but in most cases expectations coming out of seminars are often unrealistic because they do not consider the presenter's unique environment and personality.

What I am going to venture saying in this chapter—at the risk of oversimplification—is that success in ministry is largely predicated on personality. Personality is more important than the combination of structure, training, and procedural principles.

William Willimon and Robert Wilson are mindful of this in their formula for United Methodism's rejuvenation, a formula that calls for pastors to be leaders and not managers or simply maintainers of the status quo. But curiously, the bulk of their book, *Rekindling the Flame,* is given to strategy and the restructuring of organization. The authors do not concentrate on the real problem, a problem that has caused United Methodists to lose 1,500,000 members since 1969 and close 2,665 churches—a problem related to the thesis of this book. The thesis is that the most important person in the life of the church is not the denominational executive, is not the seminary professor, and is not the lay leader or chairman of the church board: the most important person in the life of the church is the pastor. If there is going to be a radical turnaround for United Methodists as well as other mainline denominations, there will need to be a transformation of the pastor.

But how does such a transformation take place? The same churches that fostered him are the ones to which he returns as pastor. Since he did not receive a pervasively religious ideology and aggressive evangelistic methodology from home and church, neither will he return with it when he graduates from seminary. In fact, because of the seminaries and colleges he attends, whatever evangelistic fervor he may have had when he got there will become placid, if not completely stomped out of him.

United Methodism is a case in point of a denomination experiencing a vicious cycle of decline that revolves around the person in the pulpit. The embryo of this decline was conceived in the liberalism that invaded the church and its schools at the turn of the century and that reshaped pastoral theory and practice. Now restoration will come to such denominations only through a radical transformation of concepts of ministry and the person in ministry. Ministers who make a difference believe in the power of the gospel radically to convert individuals. Such a belief is grounded on sound theology. There are pastors who are highly successful in Methodism and other mainline denominations, but they are either pastors who come from highly conservative churches and return to them, or they are pastors who have had such profound religious experiences that they are undaunted by the changing winds of theology and methodology.

Andrew Blackwood, who taught a generation of preachers and pastors at Princeton Theological Seminary, stated, "In pastoral work the most serious obstacles lie within a man's soul" (Blackwood 1971:31). Soul is the life principle, "the seat and center of the inner life of man in its many and varied aspects" (Bauer, 1979:901). Soul also expresses the "seat of personality" (Vine 1985:588).

The New Testament is not clear about the differentiation between mind, spirit, heart, and soul. It is clear that soul (*psuche*) is vitally related to heart (*kardia*), spirit (*pneuma*), and mind (*nomos*). For our purposes all four make up the personality. The vital relationship between mind and soul is indicated by use of the word "*psuche*" to form the word *psychology,* which means "the study of the mind and its processes." Thus the following is an exploration of the psychology of being a successful pastor and, therefore, of the soul of the pastor.

Ideology

Ideology is a way of thinking, and is influenced by the sum of a person's memories, knowledge inventory, attitudes, beliefs, and values. These can be arranged and focused by either the spirit of man or the Spirit of God. The arrangement is called the affections or desires. Desires determine the motives, that is, what a person chooses to do and the reasons why. For instance, the person who really believes that there actually is an all-powerful God with whom we can walk and talk on a daily basis and that we will spend eternity with or away from him, will act in an entirely different manner from one who doesn't believe this.

Ideology is the common ground on which spirituality and personality meet. Ideology has to do with the way a person interprets life and its events. To the pastor who leads a congregation with both love and authority, there is no doubt that God is in control and working out his purposes for the good of the church. There is no reservation in the pastor's mind that both he and the congregation are ordained and called by God. Such ordination far supersedes institutional ordination and appointment. One of the pastors whom we interviewed and whose church has gone from zero to four thousand attendants in fifteen years was explaining the organizational structure to a group of visiting pastors. In describing the hierarchy that operated his church, he placed himself at the top. When asked to whom he was accountable he quickly responded, "God."

Although most successful pastors may not be so blunt about the matter, this divine communication is sufficient rationale to knock down almost any roadblock, whether it be the opinions of a board member or the serious limitations of financial structures. A life map has been drawn by God, and the pastor believes himself called to fulfill it both for himself and the church. In the words of Thomas Carlyle, "At all times a man who will do faithfully needs to believe firmly" (Carlyle 1910:159). The failure of ministry is often simply wrapped around the lack of conviction in a cause. It is what Erik Erikson calls "The Meaning of 'Meaning It'" (Erikson 1962:170). Concerning Martin Luther, Erikson wrote:

> To Luther, the preaching and the praying man, the measure in depth of the perceived presence of the Word was the reaction with a total affect which leaves no doubt that one "means it." It may seem paradoxical to speak of an affect that one could not thus mean; yet it is obvious that ritual observances and performances do evoke transitory affects which can be put on for the occasion and afterward hung in the closet with one's Sunday Clothes. . . . Meaning it then, is not a matter of creedal protestation; verbal explicitness is not a sign of faith. Meaning it, means to be at one with an ideology in the process of rejuvenation (Erikson 1958:209–10).

Successful pastors mean to be a success for God. They believe themselves to be called to success, and it is often evident in their seminary careers. This belief is not so nebulous that it cannot be identified by peers and professors. They are enthusiastic (in God) about life and its duties. Whatever they do they do to the glory of God, take exams as well as participate in chapel, sweep the floor as

well as kneel on the floor. Ministry for them is both in the
present and future tense. Their steps are quickened by a
destiny they believe has been sent straight from heaven.
Such simplistic certitude will cause them to seem naive to
others. But mark such a person; those who make wise-
cracks about his commitment and even laugh behind his
back will soon be eating his dust. They will be eating the
dust of steps he believes have been directly ordered by
God.

One of the men we surveyed, after completing a career
in sales and attending a very conservative Bible school,
was "ordered by the Lord to a state two thousand miles
from where I was raised." The geographical territory was
culturally and climatically removed from his natural
habitat. Not only did God show him the state to which he
was to move, but also the city. According to his testimony,
God showed him the exact spot where he was to build the
church when he drove into the metropolitan area of
approximately one million people for the first time. He
believes the results of his mission, now drawing thirteen
hundred people on Sunday morning, to be directly linked
to taking orders from the "main office." Such certitude
represents a clearly defined world view.

Charisma

To state that charisma is one of the requisites of being
a pastor may be as precise and profound as saying the
sky is blue and water is wet—but it needs to be stated. In
fact, it may be so obvious that it is completely overlooked
or, at the least, presumed. The word is derived from the
Greek word *charis,* which can be translated many different ways: graciousness, attractiveness, favor, grace, gracious care, help, good will, gift, benefaction, thanks, grati-
tude. The general import of the word seems to concern
whatever good has been bestowed on the person without
his earning it or possibly even seeking it (Bauer
1979:885–87).

The word *charis* has special importance within the New Testament economy, as it is used 151 times in the Greek New Testament. The actual word *charisma* is used seventeen times and seems to refer mainly to spiritual gifts that have been bestowed on a person in a special sense (Romans 12 and 1 Corinthians 12), though there are unique usages such as restraint in sexual matters and the gift of office.

The spiritual gifts understanding of *charis* is so crucial to the operation of the New Testament church that the most dynamic segment of Christendom in our day has been designated *charismatic*. This designation did not come into vogue until the 1960s. Up until that time the churches and denominations who emphasized gifts of the Spirit were mostly known as Pentecostals (see Donald Dayton 1987:15).

The current secular use of the word *charisma* and the religious use are not without correlation. As late as 1953, Webster's *New Collegiate Dictionary* did not include *charisma* in its approximately 150,000 entries. Since the editors stated that "usefulness has been the criterion" of selection, the editors during or before 1953 obviously did not feel the word was useful enough. In spite of or even because of its overworked usage in today's vernacular, there may still be those who believe the word's parameters are too vague to be useful. One of the definitions given in the *Ninth New Collegiate Dictionary* is "a special magnetic charm or appeal" (Webster's *NCD* 1985:227). Because charm and appeal are highly subjective and relative concepts ("beauty is in the eye of the beholder"), there may be those who would argue that there is no such thing as an absolute quality of charisma.

The two primary definitions of *charisma* that Webster gives are worth attention. First, "an extraordinary power given a Christian by the Holy Spirit for the good of the church." In this book we state the assumption that there is no effective ministry or true pastoral success without the Holy Spirit and his gifts. In spite of the New

Testament's paramount emphasis on this truth, it is a theme neglected by many churches and denominations. That the Holy Spirit equips and empowers the pastor for service has been essential to American preaching, especially where the work of the church has abounded. A thesis of Hans Küng's *magnum opus* on the church is that the Early New Testament church was primarily charismatic rather than organizational or institutional. Thus the church was a living organism rather than a complex corporation of rules and bylaws. The job of the church is not to choose men who are simply capable of enforcing a constitution and maintaining a tradition, but confirming the call of persons who have been designated, set apart, equipped, and empowered by the Holy Spirit. Küng writes:

> The ministry exercised by special commission as much as charismatic ministries without special commission, is in its own way, a charismatic ministry. The special appointment by men is not simply a matter of an arbitrary decision by these men. They cannot commission whom they wish, those they like or those who suit their purposes, but only those whom God has called (Küng 1976:537–38).

Webster's second definition pertains to the sociological and psychological pursuit of this book: "A personal magic of leadership arousing special popular loyalty or enthusiasm for a public figure" (*Webster's NCD*:227). Whatever it is that attracts people and causes them to follow is charisma. The circular attempt at definition is indicated by the word *magic*. Ascribing attraction to magic is like ascribing sickness to a virus. In other words, your guess is as good as mine.

Secular management believes that the number one attribute of leadership is charisma. Charisma is the primary quality that chief executive officers look for in their middle management people, at least if they are choosing from several people, all of whom satisfactorily perform. People who get promoted do not necessarily have high

IQs or even persevere with eighty-hour work weeks. They smile at the appropriate times, laugh at the boss's jokes, and demonstrate composure under the pressure of duress. Rather than regarding them as ruthless, their co-workers generally like them.

Charismatic leaders have attractive personalities. Charisma is not necessarily flamboyancy, loudness, or dynamism. It may be a meek and quiet spirit in the midst of a sea of boastful commercialism and slick advertising. Rather than being intimidating or threatening, it puts people at ease.

Even though they may not possess the flashiness of a Las Vegas neon sign, pastors who attract people exude life. I often ask my students, especially those who are pastors, what people observe when they come into their churches, particularly for the first time. Do they perceive that pastor, usher, greeter, and choir are alive? Is life manifested in faces, voices, body language, and in general reception of newcomers who are searching for something or someone to give them a shot in the arm?

The smart pastor recognizes that he is not called to be himself. He is called to be his best self. He attempts to be exactly that when he is on the worship platform or with people in general; he is able to suppress the cares that are weighing him down—budget problems and cranky board members who criticize everything he does. He does his best to project victorious composure whether or not he feels like it. Even more important than being at his best, however, is the ability to help others be at their best. There is a best in others because they are made in the image of God, and the successful pastor attempts to bring the *Imago Dei* to full fruition.

The pastor's job is akin to that of an athletic coach or an educator: the ultimate goal is to facilitate full potential in others. Followers are attracted to leaders who can convince others that they are for them rather than simply being for themselves. At this point "the children of the world are in their generation wiser than the children of light" (Luke 16:8 KJV). Michael Maccoby argues that ideal leaders will foster in others virtues that are concordant with the times, as for example industriousness, thrift, candor, risk, entrepreneurship, toughness, compassion, love. Models of leadership in the 1980s "have developed or are developing a philosophy of management which is rooted in a concern for their workers and resentment of wasted potential" (Maccoby 1979:22).

No wonder Jesus stressed the importance of knowing one's sheep by name. Calling people by their first name is important. Compounded by a firm handshake, eyes that make direct contact with others', a warm inviting face, and a look of genuine concern are doubly important. After the pastor of the largest church in our denomination— whom I did not know very well because I was new to the group—had died, I asked the denominational patriarch what was the secret to his success. I expected something profound. His first words were, "He called everyone by their first name." That *is* profound. Calling people by their first name says, in our culture, that they are impor- tant. One is not so preoccupied with his own name and concerns that he precludes another's name and needs. That is the reason that Max Weber identified as charis- matic those people who are especially sensitive to what may be called societal needs.

Many pastors are aggressive and make a number of evangelistic calls, but have little to show for it. Someone once bragged that his pastor was the hardest working pastor in the district. That may well have been so. But negating much of the hard work was a dour, overly sober personality. He even may have been a stressed-out per- son: time-urgent, driven by fear of failure or need for approval. Rather than exuding joy and peace, this kind of person portrays a frayed, haggard tension. The invitation to the Christ who calmed the troubled sea is betrayed by the absence of joy. The nonverbalized response is, "If that's what God did for you, I think I can do without it."

Ministerial students who manifest consistent cynicism,

criticism, negativism, and just plain coldness instead of warmth need to become serious question marks for ministry unless they through God's help can dig deep enough to discover the sore spots in their psyches. A container that emits toxic fumes needs to be labeled hazardous unless it is kept in isolation. The definition of ministry is people and their need to be purified rather than poisoned. It is much easier to identify what makes people bad than what makes them good. In pastors, whatever it is that makes others around them want to be good we label charisma. Like unction, we may not very well know what it is, but we know what it isn't. What charisma is not is a demeanor and attitude that repels people rather than draws them.

Self-Initiative

The pastor does not punch a time clock. In a sense, he is always on his own time. In fact, rare is the church board or congregation that will give close scrutiny to his office hours or how he spends his time. He can structure his day just about any way he pleases. As long as he shows up for committee meetings, visits the more prominent members of the congregation who are in the hospital, and fulfills the command performances of worship services from one to three times a week, most will be satisfied. Meeting minimum requirements in a parish setting is what James Glasse calls "paying the rent" (Glasse 1972:53). Unfortunately, this is all that many pastors do. Because a great deal of a pastor's success depends on intrinsic structures of time and energy, much pastoral performance is wrapped in mediocrity and ineptitude. Such inept performers are not necessarily lethargic or apathetic. They simply do not have the inherent motivation for ministry. They would function much better at an hourly job, a job that offers external structure and security.

The ability to be a self-starter is a must for a successful

72**What Really Matters in Ministry**

pastor. There is an inherent motivation regardless of rewards and punishments, salary and promotion. This does not mean that the pastor will be oblivious to the rewards of a job well-done, and neither will he be oblivious to the fruits of his labor. At points these accomplishments will be quite obvious—the achievement of an attendance goal or the building of a new educational wing. But such accomplishment never retards the pace of the self-starter. He just keeps right on going, barely pausing to rest on his laurels or highlight his accomplishments. He will make mention of them along the way and sometimes rather loudly. But his eye is always on the next step, the next goal and the means of realizing it.

The pastor who is a self-starter is not impeded by perfectionism, one of the chief causes of procrastination. He has a healthy view of himself, a strong ego, that is able to withstand imperfection. He doesn't have to please everybody and can sufficiently withstand critics when he doesn't. Self-initiative will not be impeded by fears of polarizing the congregation. This is not to say that when the successful pastor considers a course of pursuit he will not count the cost. He will be wise enough not to initiate a program that will alienate a majority of the church members. He probably will not even initiate an action that will alienate a majority of the opinion makers. But neither will he have to receive a 100 percent vote from the congregation to start a calling program or implement some other creative device he deems necessary. The successful pastor does not act by referendum but by vision, his vision.

What gets a pastor out of bed in the morning to attack the tasks of another day, as well as persons in any other profession or vocation, continues to baffle psychologists as much as any other question. Erikson, Kohlberg, Allport, and Maslow would all give us slightly different answers. But most would agree that the answer has to do with the search for meaning. Some people search for a higher meaning, and are willing to expend more time and energy in that search. There is a strong sense of individualism that asserts, "The nature of the pursuit and its outcome depends on me, not on circumstances or obstacles. I refuse to fold and I refuse to make excuses."

Erik Erikson would theorize that a person with a high degree of self-dependence or belief in himself has successfully negotiated the autonomy-versus-shame-and-doubt age, the initiative-versus-guilt age, and the industry-versus-inferiority age. At an early age, the child was encouraged to stand on his own two feet, to explore and exercise free choice. Though the adults controlling him gave gentle guidance, they risked the possibility of his tearing pages out of a book rather than reading them, of dropping a piece of china rather than immediately appreciating its worth. The extreme opposite of not allowing the child to roam and investigate rather freely would be conveying to him constant negation, rebuke, and caution, and his rightful dignity and lawful independence would be replaced by shame, doubt, and a sense of loss of self-control.

If a child receives sufficient praise and commendation in early life rather than shame and condemnation, he will not have an overly persuasive superego to beat him back continually. In Erikson's words, "He is eager and able to make things co-operatively, to combine with other children for the purpose of constructing and planning, and he is willing to profit from teachers and to emulate ideal prototypes" (Erikson 1963:258).

Early on he becomes a worker, a potential provider, and develops a sense of industry. He learns how to achieve and accept compliments, how to fail and accept disappointments. When he fails, his parents do not allow him to blame it on the teacher, the coach, his team or classmates, or the system at large. "I am responsible" becomes his operational phrase for moving ahead in life. Industriousness is increasingly utilized as a means of getting what he wants and staying ahead. Increasingly this person is designated for leadership positions in the classroom and on the athletic field. He can be depended on.

In practical terms, what does the above mean for the person who is in preparation for the ministry? It means that the seminary student who has not held places of leadership in class, church, and community is possibly not ready for the leadership authority demanded by ministry. It means that the person who has not competed on athletic teams may not have known enough victory to motivate him and enough defeat to prepare him for the multitudes of failures he will later encounter. It means that the person who has not sufficiently participated in the workaday world, who has never had to sweat at hard work, may not possess a work ethic sufficient to support him in ministry.

It is a mistaken notion that people can be institutionally trained for ministry with little regard for their work and employment experience. It may be a cruel hoax to tell a seminary graduate that at twenty-five years old, because of four years of undergraduate academics and three years of seminary studies, he is ready for ministry. It could be that someone with reasonable literacy, grace, and refinement, and ten years in successful sales work would be much better prepared in most ways than many seminary graduates to lead a congregation, especially if he has the initiative to pick up the needed knowledge inventory along the way.

Self-initiative is a leadership characteristic of which church bureaucrats and ministerial educators need to be more mindful during candidacy procedures. Students who procrastinate, hand in late assignments, operate only by deadline, stay up all night to complete papers, are driven only by the exigency of the moment, and perform only by reason of outside pressure, will be a hazard in ministry. As James Glasse says, they don't work best under pressure, they work *only* under pressure (Glasse 1972:68).

I was a substitute teacher in a public-school system for two weeks immediately after graduating from seminary. Those two weeks are the entirety of my public-school teaching career. But they left me with some invaluable lessons. For one, they helped me to empathize with my wife, who is a teacher. Another lesson had to do with some observations I made of some students.

In consecutive weeks I taught a sixth grade on one side of town and a sixth grade on the other side of town. These kids were from similar economic and social backgrounds in a middle-class community of approximately five thousand people. During recess, one of the classes seemed to be entirely disorganized, with individuals doing their own things. The other class usually organized itself for a game or athletic event. Cohesion and purpose were self-evident in the one class, but not in the other. The differentiating factor finally dawned on me. The group that was able to dedicate itself to a common cause or venture possessed within its ranks a boy who had enough influence and initiative to effect solidarity. The other group possessed no such person. I would contend that this is a chief factor that separates one church from another in America today.

Long-Term Commitment

The pastors whom we studied signed up for the long haul. They came to their churches intending to be pastors of those particular congregations in those particular locations until death, the second coming of Christ, or retirement. They will stay at least until the Lord gives them clear indication they should leave. Rather than speaking of retirement, they are much more likely to foresee themselves dying in the saddle.

Whatever causes commitment anxiety is not within the scope of this book. It is a form of dread, in the words of Frank Lake, "that strange part of the past which being repressed because it was unthinkably horrible, exists in an unchanging present, always threatening to emerge again" (Lake 1966:207). The horrible thing in the person's past may be sibling rivalry that seemed to be constantly a losing proposition, past rejection by family and peers, lack of received affection that resulted in an inferiority or perfectionistic complex. The sources of trust, hope, and courage have failed him in the past. Betrayal at elementary levels of his familial and social world, coupled with repeated failures at academics, athletics, aesthetics, or whatever, may leave a pastor with a very low sense of self-worth. In fact, he may have entered ministry out of the motive or desire to have these areas healed. But he then discovered that the church wasn't much more friendly than the world around him.

Such a person's ministry may even turn into a contest between him and the church. He who has high commitment anxiety doesn't even want to be a part of the contest, much less know the score. He has lost so many times before, why stay until the score is tabulated or until he has to show his hand? The risk can be reduced by moving on to the next church, to greener pastures. Thus the pastor is never in one place long enough for his track record to be assessed.

One of the pastors we queried wrote, "The man who always has his eye on the next church, who is looking for greener pastures isn't willing to stay for the bloodletting." Pastors who are successful tend to stake their ministry on one church and one location for one lifetime. That may not be the reality of their pastoral experience, but it is their intention.

The pastor to whom I have just referred, unqualifyingly states, "I have committed my life to this church." Twenty percent of the congregation voted against him before he came. On his first morning in the church, when the district superintendent called for a pledge of support for the new pastor by standing, one whole section of the congregation refused to stand. He accepted the call to the church in 1982, with 450 people attending on Sunday morning and needing $20,000 a week just to pay its bills. The pastor before him had been involved in controversy and resigned from the church after the roof of the multi-million-dollar sanctuary caved in because of a structural design flaw.

To say the least, the church was in disarray emotionally, physically, and spiritually; wounds had to be healed, reconciliation facilitated, and a congregation had to be led out of disillusionment. The pastor came in with a sensitive yet authoritarian leadership style. He announced his agenda and proceeded to put it into effect. The authoritarian stance offended some of the church's members, and a flow of them left during the first two years. But the pastor was not to be swayed from his game plan. Today, seven years later, the congregation has rebuilt the church plant, doubled its Sunday morning attendance, and become financially solvent, essentially because one man was not to be deterred. He was willing to wrestle until break of day, thereby testing God and his own fiber.

High-commitment individuals love to enter the fray and stay until the victory is won. Jim Garlow, who founded Metroplex Church in the Fort Worth-Dallas area four years ago with seven people, stated, "I am on the fourth year of my forty-year pastorate. I've got thirty-six years to go." Jim, who has a Ph.D. in historical theology, states, "When I came here I found out just what I was made out of. I watched sixty thousand cars go by my location every day, and none of them were coming to my church. It put me on my face before God." Today, Jim Garlow's church is attended by over five hundred people on Sunday morning.

Deep within pastors who are committed to a ministerial location as long as God will permit them to stay is a desire to find out just exactly what they are made of. One pastor who gave his lifetime to a church, a church that became the largest in his denomination, had a rocky time during the early years. One night after a particularly critical incident, he and his wife were in tears on their knees before the Lord. In the middle of their frustration, the wife reminded her husband of a prayer they had prayed before they took the church: "God, give us something too big to handle."

Pastors who suffer from commitment anxiety never know whether or not a problem is too big for them to handle. They often leave before the weightlifting begins. They are afraid of dropping the barbell on their foot. The potential of making an indelible mark on the soul of a people and the social fabric of a community is not worth the risk of being labeled a loser. The fear of failure is overwhelming. Frank Lake writes, "Even the Christian faith, which rightly understood would enable a man to turn and stand fast against this onslaught, is oftener used to give a man strength for his flight from reality" (Lake 1966:719). The reality is this: covenanting with a people for better or worse is tough business not compatible with being faint-hearted. It is for those who are willing to endure failure after failure so that a local congregation might enjoy, even sometimes unwittingly, the victory of endurance in a world that knows very little about holy faithfulness.

Authoritative Vision

Vision is the ability to climb the mountain, look out over the horizon, chart a course, and collect people along the way. Climbing the mountain necessitates making contact with a transcendent God; looking out over the horizon means visualizing the future; charting a course necessitates the ability to navigate; collecting people requires convincing individuals that you are going in the direction that they need to go. It was said of Moses at the end of his life, "His eye was not dim, nor his natural force abated" (Deut. 34:7). One not only has to see but has to have the stamina and perseverance to carry out the vision.

A vision without substance, however, is a daydream. The fiber that provides substance for effective dreams is authority. Authority is predicated upon five *I*'s, one of which I have already mentioned. The pastor's *ideology* means that he believes himself to be in contact with a transcendent source. He has the ability to convince others that he is receiving directions from an all-knowing God. As megatrends prognosticator John Naisbett predicted, institutions will carry less and less authority as we approach the next century (see Naisbett 1982:131–57). Effective leaders are "men sent from God," and not solely from the denominational headquarters or from the bishop (such autocratic rather than theocratic appointments will be viewed as liabilities).

The pastor may not be so blatant as to implement the "God-told-me-so" answer to a complex argument during the annual board meeting, but there may be many subtle ways of hinting that he is a man who is on God's frequency. There is a high likelihood that from the very beginning both church and pastor will be convinced that their relationship was and is a marriage made in heaven. The call of the pastor to that particular location will have been preceded by much prayer and waiting on God.

Secondly, authority is built on *identification*. He is a man of the common touch. There is no veneer of education or sophistication that hides the fact that he hurts, bleeds, and puts on his pants just like everyone else. He knows how to rejoice with those who rejoice and weep with those who weep. Americans demand that their leaders be a part of the "common lot." "If you haven't been where I have been, how can you tell me where I need to go?" Christ set the pattern as "representative man;" the Book of Hebrews says, "For this reason he had to be made like his brothers in every way, in order that he might become a merciful and faithful high priest in service to God" (Heb. 2:17). In spite of Christ's being in constant touch with the Father, loftiness and detachment were dispelled by his being born in a manger and riding on a donkey. This rare combination also made Abraham Lincoln the American prototype for leadership, as expressed by George W. Bell's lines: "A man our very own, / to earth so near, / So simple in his heartfelt tenderness / yet with a vision piercing heights, a seer" (see Capps 1977:261).

Vision from the mountain tops will be perceived by persons who have waded through the valleys before they climbed the mountains. Successful pastoral leaders magnify their early struggles to achieve. Their preaching is filled with the following kinds of anecdotal material: "I was eighty-eight pounds soaking wet when I tried out for junior high football, and there were ten people at this church when I got here, including my four children and two dogs." They are unwittingly fulfilling a psychological premise popularized by Erik Erikson: "Great leaders know this definition instinctively, because they became great, and they become leaders, precisely because they themselves have experienced the identity struggle of their people in both a most personal and a most representative way" (Erikson 1969:266).

Sermons on how to handle failure have drawn high reviews from listeners. I am personally acquainted with an affluent family who identified as most outstanding a sermon preached on failure by a man who was leading a rapidly growing church.

Authority is built on the third ingredient of *intimacy.* Intimacy is both vertical and horizontal. There is an intimacy with God. The pastor and deity are on speaking terms. But this does not keep the pastor at arm's length from people. He has high tolerance of people. People do not easily wear him down or grate on his nerves. He is able to form relationships with many people. There is a wider general intimacy that at times may crowd out time spent with his wife and family (this poses a real danger for pastors). One of Erikson's characteristics of the *homo religiosus* is the power to "accept as his concern a whole communal body or mankind itself and embrace as his dependents those weak in power, poor in possession, and seemingly simple in heart" (Erikson 1969:132).

Authoritative vision is based fourthly on *integrity. Integrity,* derived from the Latin word *integer,* basically means "untouched or whole." The popular meaning relates more to untouched by scandal, vice, or moral failure. Moral integrity is the lowest common denominator of pastoral leadership. A moral blemish either of the past or present will often place an insurmountable blight on one's ministry. Moral failure displays human weakness at its most basic level. The flesh has conquered both mind and spirit. Even worse, it spells duplicity of character, and people do not like to be duped. They want to believe in something or someone, and will become angry if their hopes and aspirations are betrayed by someone who is something other than he claims to be. Leaders will be more condemned for hypocrisy than for their humanity. Helmut Thielicke has said that the credibility of the pastor is a "question of whether he himself lives and exists in the house of his teaching and preaching" (Firet 1986:245).

Effective vision with authority lastly means creativity or *innovation*. One of our pastors stated that he got the most professional fulfillment out of "seeing someone really catch the vision of what Christianity is all about." He defined success as "meeting the needs of your people under all their varying pressures, failures, and successes." Catching a vision and meeting needs spells innovation. Vision without practical steps of implementation is the idealistic gas of visionaries. Practicalities without panoramic vision is the monotonous clutter of janitors. Creative leaders are able somehow to sweep corners and scan the horizon at the same time.

Peters and Waterman write concerning successful companies that "perhaps the most important element of their enviable track record is an ability to be big and yet to act small at the same time" (Peters 1982:201). Acting small means innovating ideas and techniques that work for people in their everyday lives. The successful pastor touts his church as one that will work for you. And if it doesn't work for you, he would like to know why it doesn't so that he can come up with the missing ingredient. He is constantly on the search for a workable idea. Peters and Waterman go on to write: "The champion is not a blue-sky dreamer, or an intellectual giant. The champion might even be an idea thief. But, above all, he's the pragmatic one who grabs onto someone else's theoretical construct if necessary and bullheadedly pushes it to fruition" (Peters 1982:207).

The ability to do the above is far more important than having goals or articulating a long-range plan. I recently visited with a pastor whose church has grown from ten people to almost five thousand in Sunday morning attendance in fourteen years. He adamantly states that he had no plan for the church when he came and still doesn't. He is extremely negative concerning secular organizational principles. His ministry and property facilities have "just grown." He proudly demonstrates how he started with a small parcel of land that has expanded to twelve acres through several purchases. The main sanctuary, not the result of long-range planning, stands at the center of a campus consisting of four large buildings.

The twin foci of the above ministry are sensitivity to God and sensitivity to people. Such simplistic innovation demonstrates that pastoring doesn't always have to be organizationally or administratively complicated. Innovation allows the pastor to bring the two together in ways that are meaningful for everyday people. This church has as its constituency upper-middle class young adults. The most impressive thing on the site is the educational building. The preschool section would do justice to the latest secular or commercial techniques in cognitive stimulation through recreation. The facilities look like more fun than a McDonald's playground. The giant model wooden cars, planes, and trains are there because of this man, who spent the greater part of an hour and a half telling a class that his success was based on his intimate relationship with God. Creative vision is somehow able to include within a mature mysticism the trinkets of children's amusements.

In the World

Ralph Waldo Emerson, after attending church, made this comment about the pastor:

He had lived in vain. He had no word intimating that he had laughed or wept, was married or in love, had been commended, or cheated, or chagrined. If he had ever lived and acted, we were none the wiser for it. The capital secret of his profession, mainly, to convert life into truth, he had not learned (Jowett 1928:103).

Pastors who attract people are able to convert life into truth. They are able somehow to pull heaven and earth together. The God that they serve is interested in people's daily affairs, not just the outstanding crises of life. God is presented as a person who has feelings, a God who is willing to intervene for persons' needs, no matter how minuscule they may seem to others. The successful pastor accomplishes this conversion of life into truth in several ways.

Lifestyle

The pastor does not live in a cloister. He lives, breathes, jogs, plays handball, goes skiing, golfs, collects stamps, or does any one of dozens of things people do in their spare time. He averages almost five hours of recreation a week, which is probably as much as the average person, at least if one subtracts watching TV. He also averages over four hours of exercise a week, which is a favorable comparison with other professionals. The pastor is perceived as one who recreates as well as labors, one who sweats as well as prays.

When 65 percent of the surveyed pastors defined evangelism as lifestyle, they no doubt had in mind freedom from hypocrisy and inconsistency. But they meant something other than a model on display marked by a sign that says, "Do not touch." Such a stance smacks of artificiality rather than the genuineness of life's give and take. Confidence in the pastor's emotional stability and his ability to identify with his species is important for persons seeking a spiritual leader. The double standard that places the pastor on a different plane of existence from ordinary folk may produce well-defined theological nuances, but it will be detrimental to his ministry.

One-on-One Dialogue

The successful pastor is not only an articulate speaker in the pulpit, but an ardent listener in private conversation. He has a sincere interest in where his people are coming from, where they desire to go, and the obstacles that keep them from getting there. He relates to life, because he listens to the heartbeat of those around him. Heartbeats are quickened by the finding of a lost coin and a lost sheep as well as the salvation of a lost sinner. He is not oblivious to those things that occupy the thoughts and energies of others, their favorite athletic team, the rise and fall of the stock market, the achievements or failures of their children, purchase of a new car, or move to a new house. He allows what occupies others to become his occupation. The capacity to absorb such a multitude of concerns and to inquire about them at a later date is not found in a lot of pastors, however.

The pastor is not afraid to respond to the confession of a parishioner, "I struggle with that, too." He walks the fine line between allowing his humanity to show and living a life of righteousness. He is not so preoccupied with exhibiting his righteousness that he squelches moments of openness between him and his parishioners. They are open because he is open. They risk vulnerability because he risks it, and there is vulnerability in allowing heaven and earth to touch. In the words of Reinhold Niebuhr, "It is certainly not easy to separate life from lust without destroying life" (Reinhold Niebuhr 1957:146). In his book, *Congregations Alive,* Donald Smith has a quotation from a parishioner that could be multiplied a thousand times by churchgoers who have high confidence in their pastors: "Bob is a real person. He doesn't put himself on a pedestal. He's just as down-to-earth as any member of the church. You can talk to him about most anything" (Smith 1981:56).

Preaching

Effective preaching is relevant preaching. It deals with where people are living. The effective preacher assumes that all of us belong to the same species: humanity. Humans seem to have pretty much the same problems; most people get diaper rash early on and earn dwindling cash later on. The relevant pastor is able to sandwich theology between the two.

Ethos pertains to the pastor's credibility as a speaker or his authority to speak. Daniel Baumann differentiates between antecedent ethos and manifest ethos (Baumann 1972:42). Antecedent ethos has to do with the pastor's prior reputation, scholarship, and accomplishments. Ninety-nine out of one hundred pastors do not have enough antecedent ethos to command respect. Most pastors must rely on manifest ethos, the ability to interpret life in the light of Scripture. The skillful insight that facilitates his preaching for the people, formulating their struggles, and articulating their innermost desires, is critical to gaining a hearing. Such preaching demands much more than linear propositional logic. It demands creative, imaginative, concrete thinking.

All too often, young preachers who have little antecedent ethos other than a seminary degree are the most philosophical in their preaching. They go for thirty minutes without ever giving an illustration from their home, family life, favorite hobby, or athletic team. Their sermons have all of the attraction of a stripped-down Yugo rather than a BMW. Dull minds stoned by hours of TV and cinema simply need something more enticing. Telling people how you and your wife handle an argument is going to gain more hearers than letting them know how to decline a Greek noun. We have to begin where people are.

The pastors who responded to our questionnaire did an

average of seven hours per week of outside reading. It should not be assumed that this was all in commentaries and religious periodicals. Relevant preachers are informed by magazines, newspapers, and television. They do not live in an informational vacuum while the world marches by. I am almost as concerned about seminary students and pastors who do not read the newspaper as I am about those who do not read the Bible. One of the most important pieces of advice that I give my preaching students is to receive a major weekly newsmagazine and completely devour it. Then incorporate it into preaching.

Long a hallmark of Billy Graham's preaching has been his use of a national or world event as a springboard to his weekly *Hour of Decision* message. No wonder people have listened to him for nearly half a century. If the Bible doesn't speak to the concerns of persons, to what does it speak? Preaching that makes sense must somehow combine the grand cosmic events with the small chaff of humanity's humdrum affairs. Such preaching demands the ability to weave universal truth into the fabric of minuscule particulars. A preacher who accomplishes this feat possesses theological imagination. Without it, preaching will be dull and boring, which is a sin the pastor cannot afford to commit.

Inclusive, Not Exclusive

Homogeneity may describe most churches. This may be a pragmatic truth, but it is not a biblical goal, and neither is it the intent or purpose of the evangelistic pastor. I questioned a pastor who had brought a church from virtually no members to sixteen hundred in about seven years concerning the church's upper-middle class makeup. He admitted to the accuracy of my observation, but at the same time protested the implication he was targeting a particular clientele. He is probably correct in his subjective observation. Growing churches and aggressive pastors do not set out to reach "our kind of people." It is at the same time true that the pastor's style and worship format, as well as other factors, may well attract a certain kind of person. Every pastor stamps his personality on the church, and that is only as it should be. All great preachers have recognized that truth cannot be separated from the vessel that conveys it.

Feeling good about our vessel is critical to our ministry. A deep sense of inferiority, paranoia, and general fear of people are self-defeating in ministry. Wholeness of personality is much more critical in ministry than knowledge inventory or practical skill. Wholeness breathes wholeness. In the words of Thomas Oden, "The very process of dwelling for a time in the presence of a congruent person is itself undoubtedly a healing force" (Oden 1966:58). Congruence is the capacity of a person truly to sense his own feelings and to express them accurately. Realistic sensing and expressing are essential ingredients for wholeness. The possibility for the parishioner to experience wholeness is enhanced by the pastor's own wholeness.

People who feel good about themselves are much more likely to feel good about others. Acceptance of others begins with acceptance of self. Pastors with chips on their shoulders, who have hostility against people in their past, who have not experienced complete forgiveness, who sense that life and its circumstances are adverse to them, will repel people rather than attract them. But the greater a person's experience and understanding of God's grace, the more will he enlarge his circle of grace toward others. The farther a person's ego boundaries are extended, the broader is his reception of others, and the more inclusive is the love factor in his personality.

A pastor with a limited number of internal threats to his psychological and spiritual well-being will gradually break down the fortress that surrounds him. Openness rather than protection becomes a mode of existence. He can accept others because he has nothing to hide. Again, openness breeds openness. The pastor who drops his guard causes others to do the same. Defensiveness repels people. Openness extends a warm invitation to others to be a part of our group, our circle, not just because we have something to give you or we want to change you, but you have something to give us. The message conveyed to others from the inside to the outside is, "You are a very important person."

Again, when pastors defined the reasons for the success of their churches and the dominant characteristics of their congregations, the words they used were *love, acceptance, warmth, tolerance, compassion, caring, friendly,* and *people relationships.* The successful pastor believes the best about his people. He projects his inclusiveness on them and attempts to move them in that direction. He is convinced that the church is fundamentally inclusive rather than exclusive and that its concern is to extend its ministry to all within its reach and not only to a faithful elite.

The pastor with the above attitude does not discount the theology of other churches by believing that "we have a corner on truth." Rather, in the words of Elton Trueblood, he believes "we do not have all the truth, but a truth for all." Neither does the tolerant pastor become latitudinarian or comparative in his approach to truth. He is very secure in what he believes. Hence there is no need to be defensive either publicly or privately. He may even be a defender of the faith in the pulpit and have very strict requirements for church membership, but the "certain trumpet call" of 1 Corinthians 14 is preceded by the bearing all things and believing all things of chapter 13. The wideness of God's mercy and the absoluteness of the truth is a paradox deftly handled by the inclusive pastor. A pastor such as Jack Hyles preaches a very authoritarian, absolutist gospel and at the same time has a wide outreach to various ethnic groups and to many down-and-outers. He is exclusive in message and inclusive of people.

Pastors who shepherd small churches are often not able to handle the above paradox. They are either so ideological that they immediately condemn others who do not share their lifestyle or world view, or they are so vague and undefined in their philosophical commitment that they offer nothing for people to grasp or hold on to. Vagueness and sentimentality are as detrimental to reaching people as intolerance and exclusiveness. People are seeking authority for their lives, which is one of the primary reasons they come to church, and they will not find it in the pastor whom A. W. Tozer called a "smiling, congenial, asexual, religious mascot whose handshake is always soft and whose head is always bobbing in the perpetual Yes of universal acquiescence" (Tozer 1966:167).

It is no accident that often the more inclusive a pastor and congregation are, the less ritualistic is the church's worship. Allport states, "In psychological parlance, ritual is a form of social facilitation which intensifies the comparable attitudes and sentiments of all participants" (Allport 1950:135). Allport should have qualified *participants* with *inside* or *regular,* because ritual makes outsiders feel irregular and highly uncomfortable, at least until they learn the routine of highly esoteric acts. Highly esoteric acts with which the "in" group is acquainted constitute a point of identity and security. It is the cohesive "high-five" of the athletic team. The inclusive pastor is sensitive to those signs that promote smugness rather than spirituality. Such sensitivity is willing to sacrifice "the way we've always done it" for the wider cause of the kingdom. (I do not mean by the above to suggest that ritual has only psychological value. All groups are ritualistic, and in many instances liturgy communicates deep theological meaning.)

The inclusive person has a secure philosophy of life. Such a philosophy realizes that God has been gracious in spite of the recipient's faults and glaring limitations. There is no legalism, self-righteousness, or moral surveillance that circumscribes the "whosoever" invitation of the gospel. Those who cling to an ideology simply because of the cliquishness and clannishness it provides their threatened egos often produce nongrowing, small churches. They have not experienced psychological maturity, spiritual healing, and biblical understanding sufficiently to release them from their prejudices and biases. They also have not experienced sufficient exposure to life, the world, and its cultures to extend open hands and hearts to people of different thought patterns, skin color, and cultural background. Small pastors and small churches at times tend to perceive themselves and their churches as the center of God's universe, rather than getting the whole picture from God's perspective. Such an egocentrism is as dangerous as believing that all roads lead to Rome. Large churches can be equally guilty.

Again, seminaries may foster attitudes in their students detrimental to their becoming successful pastors. Even if they don't overtly and explicitly foster narrowmindedness, they need to minister to those students who have been shaped by legalistic influences. They particularly need to be sensitive to students who are utilizing the "call of God" and theological commitments to bolster their own identities. Ministerial trainers need to be aware of students who have turned to a narrowly defined ideology because of past lack of trust in the home, debilitating criticism from parents and peers, and their general inability to find their places in the world of work, play, and sexual intimacy.

It is paramount that seminaries be loving, accepting communities that allow students to disclose painful areas of their psychological and moral attics. Unhealed areas of the psyche will haunt and thwart future ministry as well as alienate prospects from the church. There may be a real advantage in an interdenominational seminary that both implicitly and explicitly says to students in many ways through chapel and classes that commitment to the Christian cause is a thousand times more important than a denominational label. John Wesley, with his highly disciplined and perfectionistic personality that had been germinated in a puritanical home and highly structured environment, could write this:

> But while he is steadily fixed in his religious principles, in what he believes to be the truth as it is in Jesus; while he firmly adheres to the worship of God which he judges to be most acceptable in his sight; and while he is united by the tenderest and closest ties to one particular congregation, his heart is enlarged towards all mankind, those he knows, and those he does not, he embraces with strong and cordial affection, neighbors and strangers, friends and enemies. This is catholic or universal love. And he that has this is of a catholic spirit. For love alone gives the title to this character. Catholic love is a catholic spirit (Wesley, *Sermons*:388).

Inclusive pastors get the big picture; the world is their parish.

Energetic Optimism

Successful pastors are confoundingly optimistic, especially to people who are prone to ask why rather than why not. They reside on the sunny side of the mountain. "If God be for us who can be against us?" is their formula for removing obstacles that to others seem insurmountable. Ideology, endurance, vision, and something unexplainable in their personalities cause others to label them born optimists.

There are dangers in optimism. The tendency to disregard facts and not calculate the risks carefully enough can lead to ultimate disillusionment. Some pastors have placed themselves and their congregations at overwhelming odds by launching million-dollar building programs when interest was less than 10 percent and then found themselves stretched beyond their limits when interest went to 18 percent. Their "faith" got them into trouble and even resulted in their leaving the ministry. But "faith" for most of the successful pastors in our survey has clearly brought them and their people victory, to the amazement of the dozen or so other churches in town. Faith operators revel in "dreaming the impossible dream and fighting the unbeatable foe," and are likely to articulate platitudes of positive thinking from the pulpit no matter how trite they sound. This does not mean they ignore relevant facts or look at everything through rose-tinted glasses. It does mean that they serve a great God whose calling is their sufficiency. Gordon Allport writes concerning faith that provides certitude for advancing:

> For all accomplishment results from taking risks in advance of certainties. Chronic skepticism, inferiority, and depressive thoughts are incompatible with everything excepting vegetative existence. The optimistic bias toward life is a necessary condition for life. Only by having expectations of consequences beyond the brink of certainty do we make these consequences more likely to occur. Faith engenders the energy which when applied to the task in hand enhances the probability of success (Allport 1950:73).

The other danger in boundless optimism is stress or burnout. A person who is fueled by optimism and excitement about the task at hand may eventually be reduced to a vapor of transitory extravagance. It *is* possible for an individual to be so consumed by a vision that he finds himself at the point of mental and physical exhaustion. But the multitude of books and articles about coping, stress, and burnout are not nearly as applicable to the person consumed by mission as they are to the person absorbed by the monotony of frustration. The person of energetic optimism soars on wings like eagles, runs and isn't weary, walks and doesn't faint (see Isa. 40:31). While the stagnated pastor is simply attempting to cope, the successful pastor is running through a troop and leaping over a wall (see Ps. 18:29).

Studies of job satisfaction and production have debunked some of the myths concerning so-called workaholism. Workaholics, unless they are driven by guilt or fear or have some other neurotic symptom, normally enjoy their work. Enjoyment eliminates various symptoms exhibited by many nine-to-five workers, such as excessive absenteeism, procrastination, and defensiveness about why they are not cutting the mustard. Inability to cope with stress and victory at the game of life are normally antithetical. Michael Posner writes:

> Success and what comes with it is one of the best methods of reducing stress. Many of us like to think that everything is not roses at the top, that success has its drawbacks: powerful and wealthy people must, underneath it all, be unhappy. Well, it just ain't so. Most successful people experience less frustration on the job, have high self-esteem, fewer financial worries, more freedom, and find greater pleasure in their jobs. Add to this that because they are seen as indispensable, therefore more attention is paid to their health, and time away from the job for regular exercise is widely accepted (Posner 1982:154, 156).

Christians would differ with the above in that the assertion does not base happiness on the absolute philosophy of life, the Christian faith. But keep in mind that it does base success on a philosophy of life: total commitment to the task at hand. And if there be truth in the importance of possessing an integrating philosophy that will crystallize and sharply focus life forces, there is unbounded opportunity for the Christian to tap unlimited opportunity. I have often noted the number of absolutes included in 2 Corinthians 9:8, especially in the King James Version: "And *God* is able to make *all* grace abound toward you; that ye, *always* having *all* sufficiency in *all* things, may abound to *every* good work" (italics added).

Those who abound to every good work need fewer diversions than others. Their work is their play, and their play is their work. There is little reason for activities that provide escape from mundane existence. The following example taken from our survey provides an extreme case in point. This pastor in four years of ministry has seen his Sunday morning attendance go from fifteen to five hundred. This high-school-only graduate spends 125 to 130 hours in ministry per week, spends three hours alone in prayer daily, and reads one hundred chapters of Scripture each week. When asked about recreation, he wrote the following:

> Jack Nicklaus (golfer) works on his farm for recreation. John Brown (farmer) plays golf for recreation. An accountant (sits all day) travels for recreation. A truck driver (travels all day) stays in one place for recreation. A motorcycle racer does art. An artist rides motorcycles. My ministry is very diverse—therefore I have much recreation!

This same pastor went on to list some of the diverse areas that provide this recreation:

> preaching, teaching, praying, administration, holding conferences, traveling, writing, video and audio tapes, physically building buildings, drawing blueprints, fasting, counseling, speaking, starting Christian schools, teaching in school, overseeing church businesses, developing new church businesses, radio station, TV work, helping farmers, cutting firewood, Christian Boy Scouts, family fellowship functions

The above portrays the person's total immersion in the mission. He has a high capacity for work and a physical makeup that demands little rest. No other person presented us with an actual list of activities, and it should be kept in mind that the average number of hours on the job for those surveyed was fifty-five. Whatever the amount of hours, however, the successful pastor uses them as energetically and wisely as possible. He is always on his own time and not someone else's, thus sensing that time is one of his most valuable resources. People who are possessors of a cause and possessors of time firsthand, normally

exhibit more energy than those who are possessors sec-
ondhand.

Energy coupled with an optimistic bias toward life and
sprinkled with a measure of common sense engenders
meaningful advance for the church. Pervasive energetic
optimism is contagious. Frank Tillapaugh states in his
book, *The Church Unleashed*: "The biggest obstacle to
unleashing the church is not rural psyches, entrenched
lay-power structures, lazy uncommitted people, or small
facilities. It is the senior pastor" (Tillapaugh 1982:102).
The correlation is that energetic optimism in the senior
pastor is the launching force that most congregations
need and want.

Meaningful Communication

A higher value is placed on preaching and teaching
than on any other activity in which the successful pastor
participates. This may seem ironic in that there are more
forms and means of communication today than ever in
the history of the world. Electronic gadgetry, overhead
projectors, audio-video presentation, as well as all other
kinds of visual aids, have done little to diminish the effectiveness of one man holding the attention of thousands of
people anywhere from twenty to sixty minutes. People
still come to church primarily to hear the minister proclaim the Word of God, though they may not have the
stamina to listen to George Fox for three hours or George
Whitefield for nine hours.

Is proclamation the absolute form, the designated
form, the paramount form for communicating the gospel?
Such a question may lead to futile debate, but there can
be no doubt about its central significance in the New
Testament, which refers to preaching/teaching 246 times.
The apostles' chief means of disseminating the gospel was
the "preaching of the cross." Most successful pastors
accept this responsibility as their *raison d'etre,* and realize that if they send the worshipers away without their

having heard how the Word of the Lord can be meaningfully implemented in their daily lives, they have failed in their most important task. They take Paul's exhortation to Timothy, "preach the Word" (2 Tim. 4:2), with utmost sincerity.

Two important changes have taken place in American preaching over the last twenty-five years. First, it is very unlikely that preaching is now regarded as an art form. Most contemporary preaching has little of alliteration, symmetrical points, and many other homiletical techniques that have been in vogue in traditional preaching. Above all there is little place for oratory, flowery speech, or preaching that is a performance or an end in itself. Preaching is a means for communicating pragmatic ideas that make sense to the listener. "He makes sense," or "He spoke to me," is a much higher compliment than "That was a great sermon," or "He is eloquent."

Closely related to the above is the second change in preaching. There is little difference between preaching and teaching in purpose, tone, or content. Some would argue that there is no difference between the two in the New Testament and that they are a singular function of the pastor/teacher. Classic definitions differentiated teaching from preaching by associating the former with imparting knowledge or information, and the latter with persuasion. Such a neat dichotomy does not fit today's pastoral communicator.

Because of fear of manipulating and a desire to protect the freedom of the listener, today's preacher is likely to be more implicit than explicit. Recommendations to particular courses of action will not be quite as straightforward as in yesteryear. This is not to say that there is no prescribed action. The hook on the end of the sermon, however, has been traded for more enticing bait, and "drawing the net" has been delegated to those few preachers who have the gift of evangelism. Nurturing, guiding messages are more in vogue than evangelistic, pointed ones. A staff is more acceptable than a goad.

In spite of not giving close adherence to timeworn homiletical principles, today's successful pastor will be able to articulate a clear message to the worshipers. He will give them an idea to take home with them. The idea will be more or less related to a story or teaching from Scripture. Open Bible, central pulpit, and placement of the sermon at the end of the service are the inheritances of the Reformation that still hold sway in American evangelicalism. Communication not only pertains to the homily, but to all that has preceded during the worship hour. Worship service and sermon will fit together as glove to hand and will reflect both the pastor's and the congregation's personality.

Pastors of large churches are able to articulate who they are and where they are going. This philosophy is reflected in their worship services and will, in turn, shape the faces of their congregations. Illustrating this is the tale of two pastors in one metropolitan area, Jack Hyles in Hammond, Indiana, and Bill Hybels in South Barrington, Illinois. Both are extremely capable communicators, but at that point the similarity ends. Hyles's straightforward, evangelistic, highly anecdotal, confrontational, invitation-oriented messages are geared to the blue-collar clientele he attracts. His worship service is in the American revivalistic tradition, interspersed with Jack Hyles's homespun humor and explicit exhortations. Everything that happens in the service is traditional. There is nothing that takes place which smacks of contemporaneity. The high point of the service is definitely Hyles's message. He volleys between the sublime and the ridiculous, which leaves his audience laughing one minute and dead serious the next. His highly dogmatic style, backed by many colorful anecdotes from his past, are in keeping with the colonial architecture of the sanctuary and the 1950s look of Hammond.

First Baptist of Hammond is a congregation led by a highly motivated pastor who considers his number-one task in life to be soul winning. He has been able to mobilize his laity and hundreds of other pastors across the nation to the same purpose. What the church lacks in refinement it makes up for in vision—a vision clearly articulated by the pastor.

While Hammond's First Baptist Church boasts the "world's largest Sunday school," Willow Creek Community Church, which averages over eight thousand Sunday morning and Saturday evening worshipers (it also has a Saturday evening service) doesn't have a Sunday school, at least for adults. In fact, there is little that is traditional that takes place here. Liturgy, hymnbooks, organ, and choir are replaced with contemporary music and drama. Bill Hybels stands behind a portable glass pulpit and presents a low-key topical message, which is biblically based but at the same time without theological terms and religious clichés. The multipurpose auditorium appears more suitable to a secular concert than a worship service. But all of this is in keeping with the leadership's philosophy. They believe that people are more apt to enter the faith via a service in "Christianity 101" than a 700-level course fitted with traditional symbols and the antiquated collections of the church.

Each of these men, Hybels and Hyles, has a philosophy and is able to articulate it clearly through the medium of preaching and worship. One observant participation in either of their worship services will tell the listener much about their philosophical interpretations of both the gospel and ministry. The worship/preaching services are foremost on their agendas, the authority of which echoes throughout the seventy-five minute Sunday morning events. Each man has a scheme and realizes that if he fails at this point, he has failed. He only has to do a few things well: preach, pray, and lead his congregation in worship. In this basket, both of these pastors are willing to place their eggs. The eggs are the meaningful elements the preacher offers his people when they gather on Sunday morning, evening, or midweek. William Willimon states it well: "For in the leadership of worship, the community function of the priest's officialness is affirmed most strongly, and a pastor's self-understanding will be laid bare for all to see" (Willimon 1979:209).

Conclusion

The above observations only tacitly concern the spiritual and theological qualifications of ministry. Instead, they provide a practical lens through which the ministerial candidate may confirm and validate his direction. They also provide handles by which a ministerial board might aid the person headed for full-time pastoral service. Providence consists at least partially of the ability of the person or those around that person to assess whether or not he has gifts and graces for pastoral ministry. Our suggested set of qualities provides a tool for that assessment.

As well as addressing the candidate's relationship to Christ, questions that need to be asked are: Does this person have an ideology that is distinctive to kingdom leadership rather than to corporate planning? Does he possess an attractive personality, the kind that makes people want to be around him? Does he have the "get up and go" that has already been exhibited in employment and academics? Does he exhibit flightiness and fickleness that do not allow him to carry tasks through to their logical conclusion? Is this candidate imaginative with gifts of empathy and innovation? Is he able in group discussions to perceive needs and ways and means to fulfill those needs?

Does he comfortably mix with people and demonstrate an ability to enter into their world? Would he fare better as a recluse in a monastery than a practitioner who can handle the affairs of life with reasonable skill? Is there a rigidity that excludes others, or is there an acceptance of people whatever their plane of existence? Does the candidate experience sufficient psychological wholeness to provide security of identity and certainty of direction? Are his attitudes toward life positive enough to produce optimism and joy rather than pessimism and gloom? Is this optimistic bias reflected in his countenance, speech, and actions? Does he articulate his ideas in a succinct, clear form, or do his spoken thoughts sound confused and muddled?

If a person possesses the strengths suggested by these questions, there is a high possibility that he will become an effective pastor. In fact, if this type of pastor does not shepherd a numerically growing church, it will either be because there are no potential converts within a one hundred-mile radius, or he has defied the odds through some mysterious quirk. The aim of this chapter has been to define pastoral success in terms of its simplest common denominators and to eliminate as many of a pastor's potential quirks as possible.

4

The Ambiguities
of Pastoral Success

*Never become a victim to the standard of numbers. In
this holy business statistics cannot measure enterprise.
A church roll by no means defines the limits of a
church's influence and ministry. "The Kingdom of God
cometh not with observation."*
John Henry Jowett

Is speaking of success within the context of spiritual
matters like mixing oil and water? Richard Baxter did
not think so. He wrote:

Keep up earnest desires and expectations of success. If
your heart be not set on the end of your labours, and you
long not to see the conversion and edification of your hearers, and do not study and preach in hope, you are not likely to see much fruit of it. . . . So I have observed that
God seldom blesses any man's work so much as his whose
heart is set upon success (Baxter:183).

Baxter goes on to suggest that those who see little fruit
of their labors should seek another place of ministry. At
the same time he marvels at the ancient and reverent
men who have persevered for forty or fifty years among

101

an "unprofitable people" and consequently have seen few results (Baxter:185).

Is it God's will that some pastors should labor among an "unprofitable people"? I assume Baxter meant by unprofitable a people who do not sufficiently respond to the gospel. But is it our business to dictate the kind of response that should take place? Because people do not join my church, respond to my message, espouse the gospel interpretation I present, does this mean that I need to write off either them or me? Could it be that a period of seed planting in a particular neighborhood may not bear fruit during my tenure, but will during my successor's?

Because my goals and aspirations are not being carried out or realized in a particular place, can I always be sure that what God wants to accomplish is what I want to accomplish? Isn't that the essence of God's words through Isaiah, "For my thoughts are not your thoughts, neither are your ways my ways" (Isa. 55:8)? The greatest realization of ministry is to think God's thoughts and follow his ways. The temptation will be to follow another path and institute new means when results do not come as quickly as I think they should. Such urgency may often place the minister in contradiction to the very God he is attempting to serve. Reinhold Niebuhr said it well: "Even the most 'Christian' civilization and even the most pious church must be reminded that the true God can be known only where there is some awareness of a contradiction between divine and human purposes even at the highest level of human aspiration" (Reinhold Niebuhr 1952:173).

Asking the successful pastor to look over his shoulder, question his motives, second guess his options, make sure he has considered every angle may be like asking the pope to reconsider his denominational affiliation. It just isn't in his nature. The essence of success includes reducing complexity to simplicity and surging ahead with a narrowly defined ideology. Forward movement is best accomplished with a telescope, not a microscope. Tolstoi wrote:

The best generals I have known were stupid and absent-minded men—Napoleon Bonaparte himself. . . . Not only does a good army commander not need any special qualities of love, poetry, tenderness, and philosophic inquiring doubt. He should be limited, firmly convinced that what he is doing is very important . . . and only then will he be a brave leader (quoted in Reinhold Niebuhr 1952:171).

Hopefully, the successful pastor senses more of the complexity of the task and the graces required to meet that complexity than an NFL fullback headed for daylight or a weightlifter training for the next meet. But then again it is doubtful that Blaise Pascal or Sören Kierkegaard would have been part of our survey. Tolstoi has presented us with our first irony. The overly intellectual, overly sensitive, overly scrupulous will possibly not possess sufficient expedience to surge ahead with the troops following. It is no wonder that Horace Bushnell called the early nineteenth-century Methodists "the shock-troops of Christendom," because of their single-eyed intensity. The successful person will probably not be oblivious to all surroundings; but then again it may help to have blinders on.

Dangers of the Successful Personality

The classic writers of pastoral care—Ambrose, Gregory the Great, Richard Baxter—had a lot to say about the temptation to pride. One is hard put to find such admonition in contemporary pastoral care cautions. Perhaps many of us sense that the esteem of many of today's pastors is at such a low ebb that we feel more like exhorting, in the words of Samuel Chadwick, "Make sure your collar always touches the back of your neck and not the front" (Dunning 1971:207).

Nevertheless, there are those few analysts of the church who warn about the cult of personality, the tendency of people to gravitate toward the person who is most appealing for whatever reason—physical attraction, mental acuity, or being a father or mother figure.

Why would there be one church in town with three or four times as many attenders as the next largest? Most of us would like to think that it is because that church has a more accurate interpretation of truth or the pastor has a closer relationship with God. However, such may not be the case. Lyle Schaller perceptively writes:

> Another perspective reflects change in our society since the end of World War II. Four of these changes help explain the increased emphasis on personalities in the church. First, life has become increasingly a relational world for many people and thus they find it easier to relate to individuals than to institutions. Second, an increasing proportion of church people are choosing to be a part of a big congregation. The larger the institution, the harder it is to relate to the institution and the more attractive it is to identify with a magnetic personality. Third, the contemporary world offers great rewards for those who can produce measurable results and then encourages bigger numbers. Finally, the erosion of denominational loyalties, which were still very strong in the 1950's, plus the huge increase in interdenominational and interfaith marriages, often means people identify with the minister more easily and more comfortably than with that denomination (Schaller 1987:34).

After a healing service that Paul and Barnabas held, the people of Lystra assigned to them the names of gods. They would have offered sacrifices to the itinerant evangelists had not the two of them rent their clothes and vehemently protested. After crying out that they were but men, they "scarcely restrained the people" (Acts 14:18 RSV). So instead of worshiping them, the people stoned them and cast them out of the city for dead. Alas, such is the fickleness of people. "Beware when all men speak well of you" becomes "Beware when all men speak evil of you." There seems to be no middle ground between adulation and contempt.

The temptation to pride by revolving people around ourselves rather than around God will not be as blatant in most of us as was the dilemma for Paul and Barnabas. It will be much more subtle. Human nature is such that it longs to live beyond the bounds of space and time. That can be done by losing ourselves in Christ; or in the case of the preacher it can be attempted through leaving behind an enduring legacy and perhaps a physical monument in the name of Christ. "In the name of Christ" becomes a front if the legacy is not in the "Spirit of Christ." The Spirit of Christ is identified in John 15:26–27: "When the counselor comes, whom I will send to you from the Father, the Spirit of truth who goes out from the Father, he will testify about me; but you also must testify, for you have been with me from the beginning."

In the following chapter, John 16, called the discourse on the Holy Spirit, Jesus refers to himself by personal pronoun fifty-four times. The Holy Spirit will magnify Christ. He will become central. This is what I call a theology of displacement. The difficulty of following Christ centers in a theology which demands that Christocentricity replace egocentricity. Personal success in the name of Christ is almost a contradiction in terms. There is a fine line between centering on the work of Christ and centering on Christ.

Are we a more personality-oriented generation than those who have gone before us? Srully Blotnick argues that because production and manufacturing jobs have decreased and person-oriented employment has increased, one of the differences between the nineteenth and twentieth centuries is that we are left with the business of "making personality more important than character" (Blotnick 1987:11). Our jobs no longer revolve around machines and natural resources but around "human resources." Note the number of state agencies and corporations now using this term.

The above has driven us to seek interpersonal relationships in an increasingly urban and alienated society. The pastor and the church can become a chief satisfaction of such seeking. The pastor most adept at relationships becomes the chief resource and model. Mutual back scratching—described as fellowship—becomes the refueling for going back out into a dog-eat-dog world. The pastor becomes the embodiment of how to pacify and calm conflicting currents of life as he stands before the people each Sunday morning. The pastor most competent in representing the "ideal self" of aspiring middle-class church shoppers gets the business. Schaller says:

> Today a far greater emphasis is placed on the competence, personality and performance of the minister. In the 1950's many members were satisfied if their minister was a committed Christian, an obedient servant of God, and obviously sincere in the faith (Schaller 1987:29).

Many denominational pastors look across town with an envious eye at a nondenominational pastor whose church is growing several times faster than theirs and think to themselves, "If I were independent and didn't have a church manual to enforce, a denominational budget to pay, and an organization to maintain, I could do the same thing. The cause to which I am affiliated is at odds with my own cause." In fact, he may actually break out and go beyond denominational boundaries for very legitimate reasons. He believes that he can define the cause of Christ more accurately and implement it more effectively than can the blunt instruments and archaic methods of denominational machinery. The institution is simply too heavy to drag behind him.

But how does the pastor keep the gospel cause from becoming identified as his cause? Without the checks and balances of institutions how does he prevent gospel proclamation from becoming personal magnetism? After breaking the traditions of the past, how does he keep the historical creeds from becoming personal agendas? No wonder the church-growth school readily admits that churches that grow do not normally cooperate with other local churches (Towns 1981:127). They believe their cause to be larger than the combined causes of the church community. In fact, they may possibly believe that their cause is larger than the combined efforts of Christendom through the ages. Will it be said about the pastors of today's large churches, as it was said about Phillips Brooks, "He was able to identify himself with a cause greater than himself, even with the will of God itself" (Albright 1961:400)? But possibly even rarer was his attitude regarding the infatuation of others: "When men complimented Brooks they embarrassed him and when they praised his deeds they vexed him" (Albright 1961:324).

The basic question, then, is, Are successful pastors sufficiently able to keep cutting the ties of people to themselves? Are they sufficiently able to direct pastoral dependence to God dependence, or do they serve as a permanent umbilical cord? Can they focus attention away from themselves, or are they simply gurus like the many other so-called spiritual leaders who espouse their personal nuances and interpretations of religious pursuit? Pastors need to keep in mind the secular observation of Erikson:

> Common men, of course, gladly accept as saviors pro tem uncommon men who seem so eager to take upon themselves an accounting thus spared to others, and who by finding words for the nameless make it possible for the majority of men to live in the concreteness and safety of realities tuned to procreation, production—and periodic destruction (Erikson 1975:165).

Buyer/Seller: Consumer Orientation

A major newspaper recently featured one of the pastors included in our investigation. The headline read, "'Shopping Center' Church Stocks Shelves with TLC." The pastor said, "We're like a shopping center church . . . where people can get all of the goods and services they need." The church accents its TLC (Tender Loving Care) program, which consists of a multiplicity of ministries, 350 specialty groups such as Mothers of Pre-Schoolers (MOPS), Victims of Rape, Eating Disorders, Men's Support Group. The pastor went on to say, "People need a positive message. Here they receive faith and hope and love, a very simple, understandable message" (Stein, *The Oregonian,* Oct. 27, 1987:B1).

The offering of such TLC by the church, which we have suggested is an admirable characteristic, some would categorize as blatant consumerism. Is the church doing anything other than reflecting the selfism of our society? Every pastor has heard these words from a disgruntled parishioner: "You are not meeting my needs." This should be taken to mean, "You are not meeting my felt needs or my perceived needs." The pastor may be quite convinced that ministering to a person's felt needs masks that person's real needs: repentance, confession, forgiveness, biblical absolutes, etc. However, few people are attracted to the church if these are prominent on the agenda.

It may well be true that people come to Christ only out of crisis, and that the pastor who can best minister to crisis is the one who has himself experienced crisis. The pastor reported on above had experienced a divorce, which partially shaped both the philosophy and direction of his ministry. There is a congruence between the microcosm of a personal conflict and the macrocosm of cultural or community conflict. A person who has experienced individual hurt is best able to minister to the similar collective hurt of those around him. But might there not be a danger in allowing a particular event or trauma to give the primary shape to one's ministry, rather than an agenda that is more theocentric?

There is also the question of the uniqueness of the church. Is it for the purpose of addressing the total gamut of human problems? Is it a medical clinic, psychiatric unit, welfare office, and recreational playground all rolled up into one? Does such a multifaceted function at least partially obscure the paramount responsibility of spiritual care and nurture, a preparation of the individual to stand blameless before the Lamb of God? Do multiple offerings give the church with all the resources an advantage in attracting people over the church that doesn't have the resources? Does this also mean that the rich and educated will define spirituality in a different manner from the poor and uneducated?

A pastor of a fast-growing evangelical church was confronted by members of his congregation for teaching from the pulpit the spiritual nature of sexual orgasm. There were obviously some who doubted the propriety of such homiletical material, and even more who felt squeamish about such family fare in a regular Sunday morning worship service. Granted, there are many Scripture texts that have to do with sex, but that God wants discussion of sexual functions to become part of the gospel proclamation is highly questionable.

The gospel minister needs to be exceedingly cautious lest he stray too far from the basics. We live in the day of self-help, self-understanding, and the constant craving of new experiences. Successful evangelical pastors must be aware that not only are their own churches growing, but Shirley MacLaine is also attracting an increasingly greater crowd, along with dozens of other self-help gurus. The ultimate question is never, Am I seeing conversions in my church? but, To what or whom am I converting people? The Mormon Church is a remarkable instance of the birth and growth of an indigenous sect: just about any brand of heresy can be marketed in America if it is rightly packaged by the highly committed.

Negative versus Positive

It is true that honey is more attractive than vinegar, but honey in straight doses can become nauseating, while a touch of vinegar may at times be exactly the right ingredient. It is also true that preaching during certain periods of the church's history has been overly negative. The bleak picture of human nature painted by crudely ranting and raving pulpit fanatics has no doubt turned many people to despair.

But there are other ways to turn Americans to despair. Not to let them know that they, according to Scripture, are sinful may lead them to other means of diagnoses. People go to an ophthalmologist to have their glaucoma treated. They go to a dentist to have their tooth decay remedied. People go to the pastor to have their sins forgiven through Jesus Christ. If that is not so, the church loses one of its most distinctive missions, the ability to diagnose disease correctly and offer a cure.

I asked an evangelical pastor of a very conservative church who worships in a five-million-dollar facility with over two thousand people on Sunday morning what he was trying to accomplish in the lives of his people. He quickly responded, "That's easy to answer. I am saying to them, 'You are a person of worth. You are important.'" There are, no doubt, people in any congregation who need that message much of the time, and some who need it all the time. But that it should be the overt message to a congregation composed of upper-middle class Americans (which this one was) may be a bit ironic. There possibly has never been a generation of individuals before ours that thinks of itself more highly than ours does.

The unique and central message of Scripture is that Jesus Christ came into the world to save sinners. It may be possible to have your gall bladder removed without your consenting to the operation, but highly unlikely; it may be possible to have decay removed from a tooth without your consenting to the procedure, but it is highly unlikely. But it is an utter impossibility to have your sins forgiven without your acknowledging them. Some people may be prompted to confess and ask forgiveness by a simple suggestion. Others will do so only after frequent reminders of the consequences and penalty for sins. Dennis Kinlaw, in his book *Preaching in the Spirit,* reminds us that the sole commandment that Jesus gave his disciples when he first appeared to them after the resurrection was to forgive sins in his name under the power of the Holy Spirit (see John 20:22–23). Certainly Jesus had in mind the disciples doing other things as well— healing the sick and ministering to the poor—but as Kinlaw reminds us, "Many benefits come from the Cross. But the first benefit witnessed by the Lord's Supper is the forgiveness of sins" (Kinlaw 1985:126).

If one were to take a poll among the parishioners of any of our successful pastors asking what they would like their pastor to preach on, possibly one of the least mentioned topics would be sin. It is an uncomfortable subject. But here is where the pastor needs to take authority from biblical conviction at the risk of losing some listeners. The man of God must never choose messages based on the popularity premise. Ralph Schoenstein in "I Hear America Polling" pointed to a book company which claimed that its "biggest profit now comes from the selling of romance novels, a literary Valium to which an incredible number of Americans have grown addicted" (Schoenstein, *Newsweek,* Oct. 10, 1983:10).

Schoenstein argues, "The dreary business of market research is now polluting the arts—movies, books, and plays." I would add sermons but possibly it occurs there in a more subtle way. The pastor cannot afford to be oblivious to the felt needs, subject preferences, and even curiosity of his people, but he must also be aware that this is a day as much as any other "when men will not put up with sound doctrine. Instead, to suit their own desires, they will gather around them a great number of teachers to say what their itching ears want to hear" (2 Tim. 4:3). Those who preach to large numbers may have even more warrant to ask themselves, Is there something in my message that is less stringent or more palatable than it ought to be?

It is the knowledge that the final veto or affirmation lies in the heart and mind of the listener that makes preaching such a precarious responsibility. One false move may cause a parishioner to scurry around the block looking for another church with about the same conflict of conscience as choosing another cereal brand. This principle is what communication theorists call sovereign audience, and what Nathan Hatch calls a free market of ideas. Preaching and theology are subject to popular vote. "This meant that uncomfortable complexity would be flattened out, that issues would be resolved by a simple choice of alternatives, and that, in many cases, the fine distinctions from which truth alone can emerge were lost in the din of ideological battle" (Hatch 1984:75).

The above means that the audience will have a lot to do with the preacher's interpretation of truth, and the importance of an issue will be measured by its popular reception. If that be so, then there will not be much wrestling with the theological complexities of *hamartia*. In a conservative evangelical seminary I am discovering more and more students who forthrightly announce that they do not believe in original sin. Why should they? They haven't heard it preached on in years and they know of preachers in the so-called evangelical camp who outright deny it. After affirming the importance that clergy have in our society, Karl Menninger, in his well-written book, *Whatever Became of Sin?*, issued this challenge:

> The clergyman cannot minimize sin and maintain his proper role in our culture. If he, or we ourselves, "say we have no sin, we deceive ourselves, and the truth is not in us" (1 John 1:8). We need him as our umpire to direct us, to accuse us, to reproach us, to exhort us, to intercede for us, to shrive us. Failure to do so is his sin. . . . The clergyman, like the psychoanalyst, must point out the truth, temporarily painful though it may be to his listener(s). As in the analysis of a patient, the preacher's words may hurt, but they hurt for a purpose, for an enlightenment, for a freeing of bound energies. The moral leader risks

being misunderstood or being understood too well. It is for these reasons that his popularity, his acceptance, his very life may be threatened. The clergyman's great opportunity is also a great hazard. Little wonder that many of those who see the opportunity lack the courage to seize it (Ezekiel 34) (Menninger 1973:198, 203).

Big or Small

There are advantages to many people gathering around one person. They may indeed receive a more thorough teaching of the Word from a person who is free to give full time to that task because he has a staff who does his hospital calling and administration. Whether a senior pastor should exclusively give his time to particular tasks while precluding others has been sufficiently discussed at other places in this work. Suffice it to say here that there are those who believe that the flock should be no larger than that which can be personally supervised and individually known by the senior pastor. Scripture could be quoted to support both positions.

The pastor should be aware that preaching and leading worship are not performance functions; they are representative functions. We preach not only to people but for them. We formulate and articulate for them their theology, confessions of faith, and prayers. We stand between their existential needs and a transcendent God. We can accurately represent them only by knowing them. Such representation requires more than a general blessing; it requires identification at the deepest levels of individual existence.

Such specialization of ministry may produce a more fully orbed program and because of that attract more people. One church of approximately one thousand people on Sunday morning had over forty events announced for the week. The panorama ranged from softball to "Mother's Day Out." The pastoral team is specialized, the events are specialized, and the groups are specialized.

While the above program is to be commended in many ways, largeness and specialization foster two qualities that are counterproductive to spiritual growth. These are autonomy and anonymity. One can slip in and out of these crowds and hardly be known. I have done it over and over again in large churches across the United States. Other than an usher greeting me at the door, most of the time no one takes the initiative even to speak to me. I am an unknown factor in a fellowship of believers. Even though the pastor believes his people to be sensitive to newcomers, my own experience contradicts this.

Autonomy means that in the larger church my religion can be privatized. Gone is the kind of scrutiny that took place in the small-town church with one hundred people. There is the sensation of a large crowd, but not the sensing that God, God's people, and God's preaching are zeroing in on me. The bigger the crowd, the better I can maintain my comfort zone. Confrontation that penetrates my comfort zone is far less likely. In the words of Elton Trueblood, "Attendance and money are easier to write up for the annual business meeting but you can never have a full report of the ministry of penetration" (Trueblood 1983:23). Again, in the words of Wayne Jacobsen, "Crowds look for clever language, human high interest, but not always for life-changing truth, especially when it confronts uncomfortable areas" (Jacobsen 1983:51).

This lack of penetration is part of what James Hunter calls the privatization of religion. The large church experience is "expected to provide subjectively meaningful interpretations of experience at the major events of the life cycle, a foundation for personal identity, and moral coordinates along which to order daily life" (Hunter 1983:14). In other words, religion provides vague parameters for living, but the extent to which the eighteenth-century American Quaker carried the "sense of the meeting" to his home and his business is part of a bygone era for many evangelicals.

Evangelicals in the early part of this century measured

a church service at least partly by the amount of "conviction," a term used to explain the gap between the scrutinizing, intimate, closely focused preaching and the lifestyle of the listener. As a rule, the larger the congregation, the more general preaching becomes. John Henry Jowett taught that "the difficulty of delivering a message is in inverse proportion to the size of the audience" (Jowett 1928:177). Jowett wrote in a letter: "The older I get the less satisfaction I find in crowds. A crowd is very imposing if it is yielding disciples for Christ. What would be the use of a huge mine if we got no ore out of it? And what is the use of a multitude if we get no jewels for Christ?" (Poritt 1925:321).

There is excitement in large crowds. Emotion is contagious. Feelings are bolstered by being in the presence of thousands of others who are of like-minded faith. To the extent that worship is predicated on suggestion and the fervor of the multitude, to that extent a spiritual high can be enjoyed. Such euphoria can be a positive stimulus for many who face a vile world that is no friend to grace. There is strength in numbers, especially when there is a confession to be affirmed and a ritual to be acted out. Psychological commitment is reassured to a person who is part of the majority, at least a large gathering of people that seems like the majority.

But in the large crowd the sensational most often lurks. The fantastic, miraculous, and magical are more easily believed. Americans who seek out spectacular crowds may be looking for spectacular events rather than truth. Experiencing an event and sorting through truth claims may not be synonymous with one another. Thoughtful analysis, soul searching, and refining of perception may all be antithetical to the immensity of a crowd, especially when the afflatus of excitement is more akin to an NFL football game than it is to the day of Pentecost. Gullibility and credulity are fostered rather than discernment and sound judgment. Exaggerated claims are more easily made by the speaker who is looking at a sea of nameless faces and more readily swallowed by the larger crowd. Reinhold Niebuhr wrote: "I notice that the tendency of extravagance in the pulpit and on the platform increases with the size of the crowds. As my congregation increases in size I become more unguarded in my statements" (Niebuhr 1957:57).

The Broad and the Narrow

Christ said: "Enter ye in at the strait gate, for wide is the gate, and broad is the way, that leadeth to destruction, and many there be which go in threat: Because strait is the gate, and narrow is the way, which leadeth unto life, and few there be that find it" (Matt. 7:13–14). There has been much debate about exactly what Christ meant by these words. This pithy admonition of Jesus has often been quoted by highly sectarian groups, groups with "high moral standards"—stringent behavioral demands in their discipline.

My own background, Wesleyan Holiness perfectionism, often reminded its members of the straight and narrow way. But those who continue to do so are increasingly becoming, to use a Peter Berger term, a "cognitive minority" (Berger 1969:6). In fact, they are becoming such a minority that they are passing into nonexistence. This does not mean that the Wesleyan Holiness groups are dying. Rather, in all of the seventeen denominations represented by the Christian Holiness Association, there are churches that have experienced numerical loss over the last decade, while many have experienced gain. The churches and denominations that are dying have continued to maintain a pietistic, separatist stance toward the world. There recently came across my desk the notification of a Holiness group in a large city, which had been meeting on a regular basis for the last fifty years, that "Because of a lack of interest and the elderly age of the constituency they would no longer be meeting." The truth is that this group no longer presented an attractive agenda and lifestyle to contemporary persons.

The Church Growth School at Fuller Theological Seminary calls a separatist, piestic stance toward the world and its ways "lift." Elmer Towns writes:

> Lift, if allowed to progress too rapidly, may also isolate the new convert from his non-Christian family and friends. The event of lift literally "lifts" a person to be more god-like and God-conscious as he matures. The process, according to Dr. C. Peter Wagner and others, is evidenced in local church life by the numerical decrease of a convert's social contacts with former friends and acquaintances after only one year. . . . Obviously, this has dangerous implications for world evangelism (Towns 1981:124).

The above statement is both right and wrong. It is right in that true Christianity (keeping oneself unspotted from the world) will remove a person from the activities and values of the world. Where the statement is wrong is the claim that this process has dangerous implications for world evangelism. It does not have dangerous implications for *true* world evangelism. Many pietistic and highly sectarian groups have vigorous and effective missionary efforts overseas. The process of lift has dangerous implications for church growth, that is, for getting greater numbers of people into the church. Such implications call for further reflection on the successful pastor's hesitancy to define himself as pious.

Thus the pastor of a numerically successful church has legitimate cause to ask himself, "Am I eliminating biblical standards that are particularly out of sync with the age in which we live? Am I exchanging biblical terms such as cleansing, purging, separation, crucifixion, and death for more euphemistic ones?" These symbolic metaphors of Scripture are not options for spiritual growth. They are necessities that bring a measure of discomfort to all of us. They never were popular and they never will be. A. W. Tozer termed the wide, popular door of the church the new cross. The new cross is much different from the old one.

The new cross encourages a new and entirely different evangelistic approach. The evangelist does not demand abnegation of the old life before a new life can be received. He preaches not contrasts but similarities. He seeks to key into public interest by showing that Christianity makes no unpleasant demands; rather, it offers the same thing the world does, only on a higher level (Tozer 1978:176).

What Jesus may have meant by his stern warning is "the broader the appeal, the more diluted the message." During my ministerial career I have had the opportunity to serve two denominations, the United Methodist Church and the Evangelical Friends Alliance. Both of these groups have had a rich heritage, but have taken quite different routes on the American religious scene. Methodism, between the Revolutionary War and the Civil War, was America's fastest growing denomination. For instance, between the years 1800 and 1810, Methodism's membership increased 168 percent while America's population increased 36 percent (see Ferguson 1971:58). Methodism is to be commended for its early-nineteenth-century evangelistic fervor. One Presbyterian in Kentucky confessed:

> I at length became ambitious to find a family whose cabin had not been entered by a Methodist preacher. In several days I travelled from settlement to settlement on my errand of good but into every home I entered I learned that the Methodist missionary had been there before me (Posey 1966:19).

But Methodism had an increasingly ugly thorn in its side. Both Wesley and Asbury vehemently attacked the practice of slavery. The early conferences of American Methodism, 1780–1800, denounced the institution of slavery as evil in unequivocal terms. In 1780 they required their preachers to free slaves, stating "that slavery is contrary to the laws of God, man, and nature, and hurtful to society, contrary to the dictates of conscience and pure religion" (Norwood 1974:93). But Methodism gradually rescinded its stand to accommodate people from both the North and South. In the words of Frederick Norwood, "The theme of reform was submerged under the evange-listic message to individuals" (Norwood 1974:186).

In other words, reform and evangelism may be quite incompatible. In 1808, Methodism omitted the rule against slavery in a thousand copies of the *Discipline* for use in South Carolina. In 1816, the American Methodist Church accepted the following concession from a special committee: "Little can be done to abolish a practice so contrary to the principles of moral justice. They are sorry to say that the evil appears to be past remedy" (Norwood 1974:187). The General Conference was indeed correct; nothing could be done if they were not going to lose large numbers of people and restrict their message for the most part to the Northern states. But just as everyone else, they found themselves in a no-win situation that soon self-destructed. In 1844, there was a split between the Methodist Church South and Methodist Church North. If the church could not find reconciliation then neither would the States.

Meanwhile, the Quakers had very limited evangelistic appeal. Winning converts to a social and spiritual cause was much higher on their agenda than winning adher-ents to the institution of Quakerism. The Philadelphia yearly meeting began seriously to question slavery as early as 1693. Seventy-five years later, John Woolman appeared on the scene, walking around the colonies in undyed clothes and denouncing slavery in no uncertain terms. By the end of the Revolutionary War it was impos-sible to own slaves and be a member of the yearly meet-ings of Philadelphia, Maryland, Virginia, and New York.

Through prayer, dialogue, letter writing, and an honest attempt to understand their obligations to God and their black brothers, Quakers reached a consensus before the turn of the century, from which there would be no compromise or turning back. This decision was not made without agonizing, misunderstandings, and instances of alienating present or potential members. Because of this social stand and other recalcitrant positions, Quakers had limited evangelistic appeal. One of the primary reasons (although not the only reason) that there are only 200,000 Friends in the world today, after over three hundred years of history, is their high visibility on social issues, issues that have had a polarizing effect in our society (FN John Sills, unpublished monograph).

William Holmes has argued that there may be conditions in contemporary society that dictate the non-compromising church's loss of members. He insightfully asks and observes, "Does the ethnic and racial mix impede our growth at the moment? If it does, then to whatever extent our society continues to be racist, we will continue to lose numbers" (*Circuit Rider,* June 1987:6).

But such social stands are not the only ways in which potential members are lost. Traditions that have been highly influenced by Quietism (Quakers and Mennonites and other pietistic-holiness groups) will experience a low degree of marketability in our age. There is a basic imcompatibility between the mysteries of godliness and a world that revolves around Wall Street. It may be that the large church owes a huge debt to the small church, at least some small churches, for being the glue that holds society together. Because of their deep spirituality demonstrated by esoteric worship, ancient spiritual exercises, and unique social stands akin to Bernard of Clairvaux and Ignatius of Loyola, they uphold a standard that holds little interest for the average American churchgoer of whatever stripe. Yet, they help the rest of us realize, if we bother to take a look, that there are alternative values that middle-class Americans have almost completely lost. For instance, if most larger churches looked seriously at the economic intradependence of church members in the Book of Acts and at the Franciscan friars' attitudes toward property ownership, thresholds of their front doors would become quite high and the back doors quite low. Middle-class Americans on the whole are looking for middle-of-the-road churches that do not demand sharp deviations from their everyday lifestyle and self-preservation.

Everyday lifestyle and majority thinking is what Marcus Borg calls conventional wisdom. Conventional wisdom consists of the values a given society or church holds important. To the extent that a pastor comes in conflict with the mores of his flock, no matter how unbiblical they may be, the less likely he will be "successful." Political savvy at some point becomes a loss of integrity. The pastor may have to choose conflict rather than loss of integrity. Christ attempted transformation rather than political and religious compromise. The conflict climaxed on Calvary. Borg writes, "The dominant values of contemporary American life—affluence, achievement, appearance, power, competition, consumption, individualism— are vastly different from anything recognizably Christian" (Borg 1987:195).

Now versus Later

A tension continues between preparing to live now and preparing to live later. At many points the demands of time differ from the demands of eternity. The preacher who best equips his hearers to cope with the pressures of American society may not be the preacher who best prepares his people for heaven, an environment where they will operate by a totally different value system. We will walk on gold in the new Jerusalem because that's about the only worth gold will have. Richard Niebuhr reminds us, "As the conception of nature to which man is always related has changed, churches and ministers have often succumbed to the temptation to substitute the needs of natural man for the needs of theological man" (H. Richard Niebuhr 1956:76). He goes on to say:

We can make far too much of the changing needs of men
in changing civilization. Religion is a highly constant
thing because the fundamental needs of men as finite and
delinquent creatures aspiring after infinity and wholeness
do not change (Niebuhr 1956:92).

Messages aimed at the here and now are much more
attractive to most than messages that deal with the
grand themes of Scripture such as atonement, salvation,
repentance, and original sin. Sermons that deal with the
stages along life's way get a much greater following than
messages that deal with the stages within the order of
salvation as defined by Luther, Calvin, Wesley, and others. Note the "how-to" messages that are preached today:
"How to Be a Better Husband," "How to Be a Better
Communicator," "How to Overcome Anger," "How to
Manage Your Money," all with appropriate Bible texts.
This preaching is pragmatic, and many times helpful, but
often skirts deep spiritual concerns. The preacher may be
tempted never to get beyond the felt needs and contemporaneity of his people. Over half a century ago, John
Henry Jowett articulated this temptation in his Yale lec-
tures:

Modern life has put on bright colours: it has become more
garish, more arresting, more mesmeric. Society has
become more enticing, and lives of pleasure abound on
every side. And all this is making the church seem very
grey and sombre, and her slow, old fashioned ways appear
like a "One-horse shay" amid the bright swift times of
automobile and airplane! And therefore the church must
"hurry up" and make her services more pleasant and
savory. Her themes must be "up to date." There must be
"live" subjects for "live" men! They must be even a little
sensational if they are to catch the interest of men who
live in the thick of sensationalism from day to day (Jowett
1928:86–87).

Jowett went on to describe apostolic preaching as characterized by transcendent themes, the voice of the eter-

nal, holy awe, expansion of mind, and depth of the riches both of the wisdom and knowledge of God. He then stated:

> It is this note of vastitude, this ever present sense and suggestion of the infinite which I think we need to recover in our modern preaching. Even when we are dealing with what we sometimes unfortunately distinguish as "practical duties" we need to emphasize their rootage in the eternal (Jowett 1928:99).

Lack of rootage in the eternal may be the greatest shortcoming in the evangelical preaching that attracts large numbers of people. The treatment of eschatology (by the pastors that we surveyed) via definition, preaching, and articulation of the meaning of success shows a woeful lack of end-time themes such as death, judgment, *parousia*, heaven, and hell.

Pastors do not sense a need to motivate their people by the allurements of heaven. Because of luxurious materialism, most of us are already enjoying "heaven on earth," and no one has recently challenged us with the mysteries of eternity to an extent that would enable middle-class Americans to recognize the paltriness of their existence and limitations of their finiteness. To speak of hell from the pulpit is almost beyond imagination. Psychology has persuaded the church that such negative suggestions will only further depress parishioners who have to wrestle with the hellishness of a frantic scurrying society. James Hunter terms this major shift in American preaching evangelical civility. In referring to a day gone by, Hunter states:

> As every evangelist and preacher knew, the horror and dread of such a fate provided not only a means for social contact in the community but, even more fundamentally, the primary motive for becoming a convert in the first place. People became Christians largely because they were terrified of an eternity in hell (Hunter 1983:88).

The ultimate aim of preaching should not be accruing benefits in this life for parishioners but preparing individuals to stand in the presence of Christ. There is no greater goal or motivation than the knowledge that all of us are headed for eternity, and that shortly. Paul wrote: "For we must all appear before the judgment seat of Christ, that each one may receive what is due him for the things done while in the body whether good or bad. Since then, we know what it is to fear the Lord, we try to persuade men" (2 Cor. 5:10–11a). Sincere persuasion needs to be out of a deep eschatological conviction.

But eschatological conviction is basically out of context with popular philosophy. The kind of self-denial, patient perseverance, and discipline the Bible espouses is not high on the value scale of a hedonistic society. Instant self-gratification and the rewards of eternity are diametrically opposed.

Nowhere is this more evident than in today's pulpit theodicies—justifications of the ways of God. God is a "good" God who never causes sickness or is never the instigator of defeat. It hardly ever occurs to the modern parishioner that God may be stripping us of temporal sufficiencies to prepare us for an eternal dependence. Is there a God who would knock the securities of life out from under us so that we might know as did Job the certainties of a transcendent existence: "I know that my Redeemer lives, and that in the end he will stand upon the earth" (Job 19:25)?

That God would have an overt purpose for pain and suffering, that it is God's megaphone by which he speaks to us, as C. S. Lewis aptly described it, is not music for people looking for instant relief. John Wesley referred to pain and sickness as "real goods" that produce happiness and holiness. Such a prescription for happiness would be considered quackery by those who are at ease in Zion. Wesley wrote to Mary Bishop in 1777:

We have now abundant proof that very many are made better by sickness, unless one would rather stay in sickness! This is one of the grand means which God employs for that purpose. In sickness, many are convinced of sin, many converted to God, and still more confirmed in the ways of God and brought onward to perfection (Wesley 1931:279).

A Case Study of Ambiguity

A church in a city in the South had once been alive and prosperous. It now found itself in a decaying and racially changing community. None of the people who continued to attend were from the surrounding neighborhood. About half of those who remained faithful were convinced that they needed to move to a more agreeable spot. The other half of the congregation, especially the older ones, wanted to remain true to the old landmark and their memories of the past. They had allowed the congregation to shrink to about two-thirds of what it had once been. How would a dying congregation finance a move to a more desirable location?

That's when the pastor of the past thirty years retired, and they called Roger Morehead. Although Roger was about thirty-five years old and had served as an associate for about ten years in other denominations, this was his first experience as a senior pastor and also his first experience in this particular denomination. Roger had previously served in a highly episcopal type of church government, but now was in a church that was congregational in its decision making.

Almost immediately after Roger arrived, good things happened to the congregation. The attendance started rising from eighty to ninety and in three years peaked at three hundred. They purchased buses and began to transport people, both black and white, to the church. Finances perked up, and the church got a very good deal on a plush piece of real estate located adjacent to a freeway about seven miles from their present location. In the meantime, they sold their building to a black group, whom they felt could have a more meaningful ministry for the surrounding neighborhood. After five years of Morehead's ministry, the church had an ideal building site and $500,000 in savings. The pastor exclaimed at this point that he was "still on his honeymoon."

Not only was this pastor progressive, he was spiritually minded. He spent much of his time preaching on personal sanctification, spiritual renewal, gifts of the spirit, and God's ability to work the miraculous in people's lives. In fact, an hour on Sunday morning wasn't quite enough time for God to do all he wanted to do. Quite often services would last until 1:00 in the afternoon because of the many people who had responded to the pastor's call for spiritual, emotional, or physical healing.

This church had historically taken a stand against the charismatic movement. But by the time Roger arrived on the scene, there were already a few closet charismatics in the church. Roger himself had been raised in an anticharismatic denomination, but was open to what the Holy Spirit wanted to do in his life and the life of the congregation. Roger became convinced that Christ meant to affect the lives of believers more than most Christians were experiencing.

The new emphases resulted in physical healings, restored marriages, emotional altar services, and more spontaneity in worship than the people were accustomed to. All this made the church fathers a bit uncomfortable. They were not vindictive in their response, but agonized with their pastor through prayer and confrontation. Roger was convinced that he was taking the church in the right direction. The older leaders, who still were largely in control of the congregation, were equally convinced that the church was leaving its theological and historical moorings. Roger and the conventional wisdom of the church were in conflict.

After about a year of the tension, both Roger and the church fathers were concerned that the church might split. Thus they amicably decided that Roger would resign the church, and if there were those who wanted to follow him they were free to do so. So at the end of year six, Roger walked away from a new church site, a half million dollars in the bank, and a church that had just appeared to be on the verge of the greatest moment in its existence. Roger, a seminary graduate, now works full time in a bakery trying to support his family, while he shepherds the twenty people who followed him. One would be hesitant to apply the word *success* to Roger at this point of his pastoral experience, unless the word be compatible with "conviction of purpose." Alas, if only Roger had had a continuing education course in "conflict management." But then, that was Martin Luther's problem.

Conclusion

Rarely is success purely or simply defined. There is an Aristotelean, delicate balance between virtue and vice. A person rarely accomplishes a goal without negating other values that may have been equally important. Success often comes at the expense of sacrificing relationships and opportunities. In retrospect they may seem more important than when they were trampled over in the pursuit of superficially defined goals.

I heard a pastor of the largest church in his denomination tell of his high commitment to ministry. He spends fifty hours in his study per week and an additional fifty hours doing the work of pastoral care. He is a person with supercharged energy as well as highly visible ministry gifts. But did he experience even a prick of his conscience that he might be imposing on his seminar listeners a standard that is unique to him and beyond their accountability? Did anyone ask him if he was easy for his wife to live with, and was there assurance about the nurture he had given to his children?

Success needs continual redefining and fine tuning and perhaps, even with that, not all ambiguity will be erased.

A definition of success is not something that can be settled for all time and all ages. What one age scorns, another idolizes. Little did the Roman soldiers know when they drove spikes through the flesh of Christ that the cruelest form of execution would one day become the foremost symbol in the world. Success replaces failure and failure replaces success at the whim of public opinion. Anyone who receives an accolade either from his peers or from the masses should, in the midst of his elation, repeat at least once these words of Jesus: "Woe unto you, when all men speak well of you" (Luke 6:26).

5

Tracing Success in the American Church

But people are curious about the result, as they are about the result in a book—they want to know nothing about dread, distress, the paradox. They flirt aesthetically with the result, it comes just as unexpectedly but also just as easily as a prize in the lottery; and when they have heard the result they are edified. . . . It is abhorrent to my soul to talk inhumanly about greatness, to let it loom darkly at a distance in an indefinite form, to make out that it is great without making the human character of it evident—wherewith it ceases to be great.

Sören Kierkegaard
Fear and Trembling

Though they were contemporaries, Charles G. Finney had never heard of Sören Kierkegaard; neither had the rest of the nineteenth-century American public. The Danish philosopher was even further removed philosophically from Americans than he was geographically. But Finney was prototypically American in both thinking and style. Finney wrote:

Show me a more excellent way, show me the fruits of your ministry, and if they so far exceed mine as to give me cre-

dence that you have found a more excellent way, I will
adopt your views. But do you expect me to abandon my
own views and practices, and adopt yours when you your-
selves cannot deny that, whatever errors I may have fall-
en into, or whatever imperfections there may be in my
preaching, in style and in everything else, yet the results
justify my methods (Finney 1876:83).

Which of the above two Christians has had more influence on American religion there is no doubt. The peaks of
the nineteenth century that American evangelicals consider their operational points of reference are the antebel-
lum Finney era and the postbellum D. L. Moody era. The
latter succinctly said, "It makes no difference how you get
a man to God, provided you get him there." The sermon
that got the most visible results was inherently the best.

Growth as a Criterion for Success

Nineteenth-century evangelistic and revivalistic preaching was far removed from the theological homilies of the
seventeenth- and eighteenth-century Puritans. Bringing
about the experience of conversion became more important than right theological reasoning. Demonstrable
results replaced interpreting the exigencies of life within the context of God's holy sovereignty. Edward M.
Collins, Jr., writes, "Whether a sermon was homiletical-
ly a work of art was no longer the criterion. A sermon
now was judged by the effect. Style was secondary to
conversion. Organization gave way to immediacy"
(Collins 1969:115).

Throughout the eighteenth century, with more denominations and sectarian groups, more diverse theology, and
a rapidly expanding frontier, increasing attention was
given to a preacher who could increase the number of
people for his particular group and cause. Donald Scott in
his meticulously researched work, *From Office to
Profession,* states that "by the nineteenth century congre-
gationalism had begun to place far greater value on a

clergyman's performance as a preacher than upon the benefits to be gained by the simple presence of a settled minister" (Scott 1978:119).

Indeed, the results of preaching were far easier to measure than theological debate or soul care. Not that the methods of the "great" evangelists and preachers were without theological underpinning. Right preaching meant right theology, and right theology meant conversion, and conversion meant heaven, and heaven was certainly a worthy goal; but preacher and goal often collapsed into one another, and legitimacy in one was legitimacy in the other. Americans less and less believed that there were certain people predestined for heaven. They placed increasing emphasis on persuasion and decreasing emphasis on providence. Dwight L. Moody said he was an Arminian up to the cross, but a Calvinist beyond.

The American population grew, the denominations multiplied, and the competition for souls became keener. If heaven validates conversion, and conversion validates the truth, then the preacher who converts the most is the preacher whom God smiles on, since God loves truth. In no country was truth more competitive than in nineteenth-century America. Sidney Mead summarizes the above historical perspective when he states that the volunteerist churches and the rapidly expanding frontier "worked to intensify the sense of competition between the free, absolutistic groups in the vast free market of souls—a competition that helped to generate the tremendous energies, heroic sacrifices, great devotion to the causes, and a kind of stubborn plodding work under great handicaps that transformed the religious complexion of the nation" (Mead 1977:103).

The Wesleyan Influence

The above scenario has not been limited to the development of the American church. John Wesley was the forerunner of and model for much of the evangelistic and revivalistic thrust that took place in America before the Civil War. During approximately fifty years of preaching an evangelical gospel in England, he and his preachers won seventy thousand converts to the Methodist cause. Wesley noted his "strangely warmed heart" experience at Aldersgate Street on May 24, 1738, as the watershed of his ministry. According to his own testimony, his preaching with little results was transformed, and "the word of God ran as fire among the stubble; it was glorified more and more; multitudes crying out, 'What must we do to be saved?'" (Wesley 1958:469).

Wesley justified his ministry by pointing to results, especially when he was at odds with his ecclesiastical superiors. To the chaplain of the Earl of Dartmouth he wrote, "I would observe every punctilio of order except where the salvation of souls is at stake. There I prefer the end before the means" (Wesley 1931:146). He defended field preaching by noting that in 1759 "greater numbers than ever attend" (Wesley 1938:354). To defend his journeys into and evangelistic labors in other pastors' parishes, John Wesley noted "the number of persons on whom God has wrought" (Wesley 1938:122). But he also noted the quality of the spiritual work, pointing to "the depth of it in most of these, changing the heart as well as the conversations" and "the continuance of it" (Wesley 1938:122).

John wrote to his brother Charles on April 26, 1772: "Your business as well as mine is to save souls. When we took Priest's orders, we undertook to make it our business. I think every day lost which is not (mainly at least) employed in this thing" (Wesley 1958:139). Does John's charge to his brother Charles represent a unique departure in the history of *cura animarum* (cure of souls)? Had any other major figure in the church made soul care synonymous with soul winning? One would be hard put to find a historical statement anywhere within the previous seventeen hundred years that had put the matter so succinctly. Wesley's defining soul winning as the essence of ministerial labors may have been his most lasting contribution to the evangelical revival. As Skevington Wood capably argues, John Wesley was first and foremost an evangelist (Wood 1978:147).

American Methodism

John Wesley's expediency was transatlantic and provided the mantle for Francis Asbury and the pioneer itinerants of early American Methodism. The voluminous literature by and about Francis Asbury underscores his imprint upon America and the early Methodist Church. He rode on horseback 270,000 miles, crossed the Alleghenies over 60 times, preached 16,500 times, and ordained 4,000 men. When he came to America in 1773, there were 600 Methodists; when he died in 1816, there were over 200,000. His journal, giving close account of his Herculean efforts, is the best and most complete American travelog written before the Civil War.

But most of the converts of America's fastest growing denomination came one by one, two by two, or family by family. Although camp meetings were utilized, they were not as strategic as previously supposed. In the early nineteenth century, the typical camp meeting would have been large at one hundred people, and only a few of those present would have been numbered among the unconverted. Conversion came not through mass appeal but through the establishment of thousands of small churches in small communities—in some cases on the frontier in the middle of nowhere.

Such evangelistic outreach and growth came at great personal sacrifice. Ivan Howard, in a meticulous study, reminds us that "nearly half of the itinerants who had died by 1847 were less than thirty years of age" (Howard 1965:5). James Finley, one of Methodism's first historians, wrote, "There was nothing in those days to render an itinerant life in the least degree enticing" (Howard 1965:11). Able Stevens, editor of *The Methodist,* says, "The system speedily killed off such as were weak of body, and drove off such as were feeble in character" (Howard 1965:5). By 1800, 650 ministers had agreed to the itinerant system, which meant possibly going on a circuit half the size of Michigan, four or five hundred miles from the closest Methodist, simply at the suggestion of Asbury.

Efficiency Models for Ministry

Such prodigious labors as the above are far removed from the efficiency models for evangelism established in the latter nineteenth and early twentieth centuries. X number of dollars spent at Y spot for Z number of days yielding XYZ number of converts was a neat equation. In the 1880s, an evangelist argued that his efforts were much more cost effective than Dwight L. Moody's, because the latter had produced converts at $7.43 apiece, while his competitor could guarantee conversions at $4.92 each (Weisberger 1958:240). The consumer model was to have an increasingly prominent part in American evangelism.

It may have been impossible for Americans to escape such producer-consumer type thinking when they were in an industrial revolution. Efficiency and truth became one and the same. At the dawn of the industrial age, a pastor wrote his son who was in the ministry:

> I do not suppose that the exact degree of a minister's fidelity or skill in dividing the word of truth, can be measured by the number of conversions in his parish, nor even that uncommon success in "winning souls to Christ" is a certain evidence of his personal piety. But I think it is an evidence that he preaches the truth (quoted in Mead 1956:229).

As America increasingly became the progenitor of bigness, productivity, competition, and bottom-line success standards, is it reasonable to believe the church would have escaped the predominant American thinking of the last one hundred years? Robert Bellah argues that for most Americans the standards for success are consumption and income, which launches people into a sea of relativity (Bellah 1985:76). The spiraling affluence of their neighbors is the only standard by which they can judge themselves. Such standards are often extrabiblical and sometimes downright immoral, but they are clearly and easily defined and for Americans are the fiber of opportunism and justice. If one is going to beat someone else fairly, must not there be objective standards for rewards and punishments, kudos and reprimands? Should the pastor's tenure at a church be based on anything different from that of a manager of a plant or the president of a college?

Changed Expectations of the Pastor

Donald Scott has traced the change that took place in New England ministry from 1750 to 1850. In the 1700s, the ideal pastor had grown up in the community where he served, had demonstrated spiritual gifts and maturity, and had quite likely been raised in a ministerial family. The longer he stayed in the community and the more faithfulness he demonstrated in the day-by-day *cura animarum*, the more prominence he held in the eyes of the people. Before 1750, the individual pastor in a single community was its most prominent resident and a member of the highest professional class in America. He was probably the best-read, best-educated, most articulate person in the community, and he was very likely to spend all of his ministerial career in that one place. He was indeed a town fixture. His prominence depended on his stability and permanence.

After 1800, the settled, sedentary pastor was contrasted with a new breed of minister. The new breed was itinerant and did not possess the transparency that comes by year after year ministering to the same people. And he could provide more tangible results. Where edification and providing the people with a Weltanschauung to cope with life had been the primary tasks of ministry, it was now visiting evangelists who "established models of intensity and effectiveness that the regular stated pastor could not maintain" (Scott 1978:119). The later nineteenth century saw new developments in ministerial components: oratorical skills, evangelistic results, successively larger pastorates, social activism, speaking on national issues, and usefulness in the greater evangelical cause.

A prototype for the new breed was the itinerant evangelist Peter Cartwright. Cartwright's charisma consisted of indefatigable physical stamina, quick wit, uninhibited boldness, and above all, identification with the common man. Katherine Dvorak points to the extemporaneous, anecdotal and participatory style of Cartwright's preaching (Dvorak 1988:120). Cartwright's dependence on the Holy Spirit and his expectation of the miraculous and instantaneous transformation of others contrasted with the learned methodical nurturing of settled ministers. Dvorak writes: "Charismatic domination is guided by inspiration and revelation, not reasonable rules and time-honored traditions. It is irrational and revolutionary. Cartwright often shocked those around him with unconventional but charismatically consistent behavior" (Dvorak 1988:121). Such behavior was in keeping with the times.

But a different kind of ministerial charisma arose at the beginning of the twentieth century. It was far more rational than Cartwright's spontaneity and was more fitted to an urban industrialism than a frontier mentality. E. Brooks Holifield traces the transition from self-denial to self-expression in his excellent work, *A History of Pastoral Care in America*. There was an increasing emphasis on the pastor having a good personality, qualities of salesmanship, masculine traits, and resemblance to "the vice-president of a small but booming enterprise" (Holifield 1983:217).

Organizational loyalty, administrative skills, and the ability to market the product would pay off in status and prestige for both pastor and church. Increasingly "books and manuals instructed the clergy in how to advertise their teaching, improve their Sunday School attendance, build their congregations, solve their problems, and achieve success" (Holifield 1983:218).

Finding a Biblical Norm
Within Cultural Parameters

Whether American culture is molding the church or vice versa is debatable. Accommodation by the church is inevitable, and some would even argue necessary, if the church is going to appeal to our society. At any rate, the church, just as any other institution, seems to be bent on finding the most effective way to accomplish something in terms of time, energy, and money. If the least produces the most, the procedure is almost beyond criticism. Dr. E. S. Anderson, growth consultant for the Sunday School Board of the Southern Baptist Convention writes:

> The only denomination in the history of Christianity to enroll over 7,000,000 people and teach 3,500,000 of these each week in Sunday School is the Southern Baptist Convention. The methods and organizations used to accomplish this are fundamental. Some of these have been questioned by critics, but until someone reaches more people for Christ, for Bible study, and for salvation, I do not feel that there are any valid criticisms (Towns 1981:170).

Not all evangelicals agree with such a simple assessment. J. I. Packer fears that such a teleological measurement belittles the sovereignty of God and sensitivity to the Holy Spirit. Aiming at particular results based on pragmatic goals thwarts day-by-day Christian obedience. Such a simplistic measure of success clouds the Christian's complex need to take a Christian stand in a world that lives by a sub-biblical standard.

But who would argue that the eternal salvation of as many people as possible is not a worthy goal? Proverbs 11:30 states, "He who wins souls is wise." Would not the corollary to that be, "He who wins the most souls is the wisest?" How could there be more inherent value in being the very best in the highest occupation? Is this not the purest form of existence? Since the values of our society are so divergent and so misconstrued, the minister has the opportunity to reach the mark of the high calling of God in Christ Jesus, a mark at least tacitly agreed on by a very large segment of American society, the so-called evangelicals.

A large proportion of our society has turned to pursuits where winning and losing are easily defined. Sociologically and psychologically we desire little ambiguity in assessing the final score. This is seemingly the need for a person to state, "I won and I win a certain percentage of the time. My record speaks for itself." Such a simplistic philosophy of life lends itself to our sports-crazed society. Norman Podhaetz wrote in 1972:

> The major preoccupation . . . is to do something supremely well in which everyone has agreed that this is the major objective and in which the better the person or team does something, the more honor and the more and greater riches are likely to accrue to him. We want that kind of world, we see it in less and less pure form in other areas of our national life. The need and the hunger for such a world is what accounts for the passion that so many people, including me, feel about professional sports (quoted in Novak 1976:115).

Can the pure form of winning or losing in sports or economics be transferred to the sphere of ministry without its being overly accommodating to our culture? Even more importantly, will such a game plan, while producing the greatest number of "Christians," produce a "Christian" who is less than Christian? Opinions abound on all sides. Vernon Grounds indicts American evangelicalism for its "standards of success which are utterly nonbiblical," and states that the superchurch cult is "tied to the success syndrome of American business and its pastor can become like the chief executive of a corporation. Growth is the bottom line of the superchurch, and this puts enormous pressure on the church to measure itself with a different measuring stick than God has" (Grounds 1986:35).

While for many, Grounds's accusation would be overly harsh and generalistic, his tying of the church to Madison Avenue techniques is not without foundation. For instance, leaders of a major evangelical denomination urged their pastors to read the 1985 best seller advising American corporations, *In Search of Excellence* (*Christianity Today,* Feb. 15, 1985:55). This pursuit of secular management principles is not an isolated case. There is the deepening conviction that no matter how good your product, it must be properly marketed, and that includes God. You must have a rational, marketable strategy for winning the neighborhood and eventually the world for Jesus. In his carefully researched sociological study of evangelicals, James Hunter points to the precisely packaged "steps, laws, codes, and guidelines" for evangelism and church growth. He lifts the following material from Campus Crusade founder Bill Bright as a case in point:

> God's Plan was our first written "how-to" material—that is, material which explains simply and specifically how an individual can arrive at a desired goal, and also how he, in turn, can help others to arrive at the same goal. The "how-to" approach is one of the most needed and most powerful approaches to the Christian life and witness I know anything about (Hunter 1983:75).

If evangelical pastors are going to win our society to Jesus and in turn equip others to do so, they must know how to package their message for widespread distribution. The greater the number of belief systems proliferate in our society, the more pressure there is to excel in the market competition. The only other alternative is to become, at least according to society, an almost nonentity in a sea of floating alternative belief systems. The more

140 What Really Matters in Ministry

systematic the pastor can be in training converts to reproduce, the more successful he will be. James Hunter says, "Packaging the conversion process in a systematized fashion produces effects with parallels in market economics" (Hunter 1983:83). He sees such rationality and the "mystery of godliness" as not only incompatible but antithetical. "The rationalization of the conversion experience and all other dimensions of evangelical spirituality has had the effect of harnessing the ecstatic, taming the unpredictable, and pacifying the 'unruly' qualities of Evangelical faith" (Hunter 1983:100).

C. Peter Wagner, the well-known exponent of the Fuller Church Growth School, perceives no such incompatibility between the natural and the supernatural. He senses little disjuncture between means and ends, technique and goals. In a defense of pragmatism, Wagner states, "If the method I am using accomplishes the goal I am aiming at, it is for that reason a good method" (quoted in Towns 1981:191). Although many of the techniques taught to pastors by C. Peter Wagner have been admirable, this statement is at best philosophically indefensible and at worst meaningless. Obviously my method is "good" if it attains my goal. This is the very essence of pragmatism. However, unless the goal is inherently good, the method will be inherently bad. One absurd and tragic historical illustration is that Hitler's method for annihilating the Jews was very "good," but his goal was evil, therefore his methods were evil. But they were also evil in and of themselves whatever the results. In fairness to Wagner, he is quite clear that "the Bible does not allow us to sin that grace may abound or to use means that God has prohibited in order to accomplish ends He has recommended" (quoted in Towns 1981:191).

This leads us to a critical premise for determining the degree of a pastor's success. His methods and techniques are only as good as his product. The product is defined in God's Word. If I am producing something other than what God has asked me to produce, to that extent I am unsuc-

cessful. Do the sheep only know the pastor's voice or do they know God's voice? The goal is not simply sheep, but sheep who are in a right relationship with God. The really tricky question of life is knowing what to pursue in life, rather than how to pursue it. In the words of Robert Bellah, "For most of us, it is easier to think about how to get what we want than to know what exactly we should want" (Bellah 1985:21).

Competition as the American Way

Competition is the American way. It is rooted in our laissez-faire and individualistic philosophy. Theoretically, we do not respect or reward persons for the strata of life they inherit but for the strata of life they achieve. American religion has been a foremost exponent of this philosophy. Bettering our lives here and now has been assigned biblical proof texts by many evangelicals who have been molded by people who were less than biblical. Bellah writes, "In short, Benjamin Franklin gave classic expression to what many felt in the eighteenth century—and many have felt ever since—to be the most important thing about America: the chance for the individual to get ahead on his own initiative" (Bellah 1985:33). Getting ahead on our initiative not only has been synonymous with the American spirit but with "Christianity" as well. Walter Laurence wrote in 1901, "Godliness is in league with riches . . . the race is to the strong" (Laurence 1966:328).

Intra-church competition and inter-church competition have been part of ecclesiastical life for at least a century. Moody rewarded his street urchins with candy and field trips for filling up pews with their friends. All of us have been in a city or denomination where church A had a "friendly" Sunday school attendance contest with church B. There are few church groups who have scruples against handing out plaques and certificates at their annual conferences for most increased membership or attendance. These rewards rarely note the extenuating circumstances surrounding the pastor's success. Neither are awards given to the pastor who has persevered against the most negative circumstances and has somehow managed to maintain both sanity and faith in God. Is it possible to define success in terms of a competitive ecclesiastical market? John Francis Kavanaugh raises a red flag with his statement,

> Earning salvation, winning salvation, proving that we are good, competing for salvation, marketing salvation, selling salvation, guaranteeing salvation, are not only common expressions of the commodified gospel. They are rejections of the Gospel of Jesus (Kavanaugh 1981:89).

Many pastors are surrounded by upwardly mobile, middle-class people. Is it any accident that concentrations of large churches are found in such upwardly mobile, executive-oriented areas as southern California, Phoenix, and the urban areas of Texas? While some of these areas have the largest concentrations of megachurches, they are at the same time some of the least-churched areas in America. Santa Clara County, which makes up a large part of what is known as Silicon Valley in northern California is a prime example. The county boasts six churches with congregations of two thousand members, but if every church of whatever stripe were filled on Sunday morning, they would house only 11 percent of the Anglo population (R.I.S.E.:1986). There never has been a time in American church history when a geographical area so underchurched could boast of so many super-churches.

Measuring Ministerial Success

"Successful" American pastors are surrounded by "successful" American people. The essence of success according to most Americans is upward mobility. Robert Bellah says, "In the true sense of the term, the middle class is defined not merely by the desire for material betterment, but by a conscious, calculating effort to move up the ladder of success" (Bellah 1985:148). Bellah argues that the American definition of success is based on an "indefiniteness," or "openendedness": the sky is the limit; one can always attain more success.

The people that the average American pastor ministers to can measure their success by the kinds of jobs they have, promotions they obtain, salaries they draw, cars they drive. And just possibly the kind of pastor they have. Parishioners have always wanted their pastors to be successful. In the eighteenth century they wanted him to be educated (not necessarily formally), faithful, and a person who had a certain spiritual aura. But as America entered the industrial revolution, the standards for success became more measurable and were more and more imposed on the pastor. Few pastors were able to retain the objectivity (cynicism?) that Reinhold Niebuhr did in his early days of pastoral work. "America worships success and so does the world in general. And the only kind of success the average man can understand is obvious success" (Niebuhr 1957:52).

It is a part of human nature to want our success to be obvious. At least part of our self-worth is based on what others think of us. Are we diligent, active, busy, persevering? This continuity between what we think of ourselves and what others think is a crucial part of our self-identity. Enhancing our self-worth through the envying or praising eyes of others is one of the chief pursuits of life. Americans think of this pursuit as advancement in life and label it self-affirmation and self-actualization. Theologians have traditionally called this overt and all-consuming pursuit original sin. Reinhold Niebuhr writes:

> This doctrine asserts the obvious fact that all men are persistently inclined to regard themselves more highly and are more assiduously concerned with their own inter-

ests than any "objective" view of their importance would
warrant (Niebuhr 1952:17).

Rare is the pastor who can break an attendance record
without talking about it. Rare is the pastor who can
refrain from asking a fellow pastor how large is his membership or how many were in attendance on Sunday
morning. These questions are much more common than
"Did you visit with anyone who was dying last week?" or,
"Did anyone confess sin in your church last Sunday?" or,
"Is God bringing moral reformation to you and your people?" The latter are questions concerning process, being,
and relationships. The former are questions about doing
and producing. John Francis Kavanaugh categorizes the
questions into the commodity model and the personal
model. The consequence of the former is to be possessed
by our possessions and produced by our products and
prompts Kavanaugh to ask, "Do we perceive men and
women as persons or as commodities? Are people of irre-
placeable dignity, or are they expendable before the altar
of planned obsolescence, competition, ideology, and vested
interest?" (Kavanaugh 1981:34).

A pastor's compulsion to talk about his obvious measurable successes is discussed by James Glasse. The only
way most preachers are able to evaluate their ministry is
by jawing on what is right with it and what is wrong with
it. There are few criteria of ministry that focus on the
pastor's responsibilities to people and his obedience to
God. Instead, pastors "speak in glowing terms about the
glories of their calling, the rewards of the ministry, how
meaningful their work is. Or they can say how badly it is
going, detailing the frustrations and complications they
confront" (Glasse 1972:69).

Many pastors find themselves on a roller coaster
between success and failure after several major peaks,
valleys, and turns negotiated within a single day. Such
frequent psychological and spiritual transitions between
despair and elation, victory and defeat can be unsettling
(derailing) to the most stable and committed of souls.

Richard Halverson raises the curtain on his experience as a young pastor. I suspect that his frank confession reflects the inner attitudes of many pastors:

> I can remember, with deep humiliation now, how I secretly longed to have a larger congregation than the Baptist Church (the largest Protestant church in town) and the envy I felt when I compared their beautiful and more spacious facilities with our meager Presbyterian plant. The sense of competition grew and deepened though I never would have admitted it at the time. I found myself becoming actually jealous because of the success especially of the Baptist pastor. How I found myself exulting when we established a larger youth group than the Baptist Church, and I took great pride in the fact that we were reaching more of the leadership in the high school (Halverson 1972:88).

Reflections on a "Successful" Pastor

He is probably the best-known pastor ever to have lived in America. He is the only person to whom Sydney Ahlstrom devotes an entire chapter in his more than eleven hundred pages of *A Religious History of the American People.* Possibly more has been written about Jonathan Edwards than any other single religious person in America's 350 years. It is safe to say that his discourse, "Sinners in the Hands of an Angry God," is referred to more than any other sermon ever presented on the American continent.

Jonathan Edwards made Northampton, Massachusetts, the center of American Christendom. After he preached a series of messages on the sovereignty of God, to his surprise a revival broke out in his church. As Edwards worked through his theme, "Man is nothing; God is all," a steady stream of converts during 1734–35 raised church attendance to approximately three hundred. The meeting house was overflowing, and on Christmas 1737, Jonathan Edwards dedicated a new church at the center of Northampton. Not only was it at the center of this New England village, but it was also the best-known church in America. Its influence jumped the Atlantic when John Wesley read Edward's *Narrative of the Surprising Work of God in the Conversion of Many Hundred Souls in Northampton and Neighboring Towns and Villages,* which had been written in 1737. Wesley exclaimed, "Surely this is the Lord's doing, and it is marvelous in our eyes" (Ahlstrom 1975:302).

In spite of such obvious success, everything did not go well with Edwards's ministry. For one thing, Edwards was convinced that his salary was inadequate. In the words of Ola Elizabeth Winslow, "He had a houseful of children; there was much illness; more servants were necessary; he was buying books, pastures, sheep; the budget would not balance" (Winslow 1973:216). The expenditures of the family came under close scrutiny. There were tense feelings between the pastor's family and the church throughout the 1740s. Some requests for expenses, because they were felt to be too lavish, were outright denied by the congregation.

Other than the ongoing tension, the first real crisis took place in pastor-parish relations in 1744. A midwife instruction book was being circulated by the young people, and Jonathan Edwards decided he would meet the "carnal lust" of the offenders head on. He read off a list of the suspects before the congregation, without fear or favor, which touched some of the leading families. Some were firmly convinced that this was a matter for parental authority and not ecclesiastical intervention. The case of the book was quickly resolved, but the pastor-parish relations were irreversibly damaged. The revival of ten years before had now dissipated into spying, gossiping, and whispering. The sexual curiosity of some boys on the fringes of the church had turned into a religious scandal. An investigation that could have been conducted quietly behind closed doors became Northampton's dirty laundry for the glaring eyes of all New England.

But the straw that broke the camel's back was Edwards's doing away with the "Half-way Covenant" in the Northampton church. Solomon Stoddard, Jonathan Edwards's grandfather, had decided to allow the nonconverted members of the church, the half-convenanted, to enjoy the benefits of Holy Communion. But in Edwards's thinking it was not enough simply to have been baptized under the auspices of parents and church; one must be converted by God to eat at his table. Such was in keeping with the full tenor of Edwards's teaching and preaching.

Never mind that Edwards's actions were completely consistent with his theology concerning the need for "holy affections"; the die had been cast. The church dismissed him after twenty-three years of faithful ministry: 230 votes against him and 23 for him. In his own words, he had spent "the prime of my life and strength in labours for your eternal welfare" (Winslow 1973:258). When he spoke these words in his farewell sermon, he probably had no premonition of how true they were. The next six years before his death in 1757 were spent at an Indian outpost called Stockbridge, a project sponsored by the Society for the Propagation of the Gospel. Edwards was not only culturally unfit and physically handicapped for the venture, but he never learned the Indians' language sufficiently to preach in their native tongue. The problems of Edwards's personal idiosyncrasies were compounded by divisions among the Indians and dissension among the dozen or so families that lived at Stockbridge for the purposes of the mission.

Increasingly, Edwards escaped the insurmountable problems of his ministry by turning to theological and philosophical pursuits. During this time he wrote the treatises *The Freedom of the Will, The Great Christian Doctrine of Original Sin,* and *The Nature of True Virtue.* At the time of his call to Princeton, he was working on possibly his most monumental task, *History of the Work of Redemption.* He became president of the college on February 16, 1758. A little over a month later he was dead. Even though cut down in midcareer, "he was one of the most prodigiously productive thinkers of the age" (Ahlstrom 1975:311). His philosophical mind, which sacrificed itself to deep religious conviction, rendered Edwards a "failure" in ministry, but at the same time left for America an enduring legacy of spiritual pursuit and theological understanding.

Conclusion

Jonathan Edwards was possibly a victim of his own success. His parishioners perceived that their pastor's glowing reputation of earlier days and the increasing recalcitrance of his convictions as incompatible. His attempts to keep his conscience void of offense and their ideas of ministerial effectiveness came into conflict. Indeed, there may often be tension between the claims of truth and popularity. The American church has not always demonstrated keen awareness at this point.

This chapter has attempted to trace the development of growth, competition, widespread distribution of the message, and evangelistic results as the parameters of success in the American church. We have not presumed that these are the biblical absolutes of ministry. While it helps to gain a historical understanding and formulate contemporary handles of effectiveness, one needs to search the scriptures for principles which are good for all times and places. We believe that universal definitions of effective ministry can be garnered from biblical models. This we will proceed to do in the next chapter.

6

Defining *Success* Biblically and Christologically

We are henceforth to worship defeat, not victory; failure, not success; surrender, not defiance; deprivation, not satiety; weakness, not strength. We are to lose our lives in order to keep them, to die in order to live.
Malcolm Muggeridge
Jesus Rediscovered

The scholars who worked under the auspices of King James I in the early seventeenth century chose to use the word *success* in one place in the entire Old Testament. It is a translation of the word *sakal* (Brown, Driver, and Briggs [BDB] 1972:968), which carries more of the connotation of prudence, insight, comprehension, and understanding than it does the twentieth century understanding of success. *Sakal* is in all other places in the Old Testament translated "wise" (Dan. 12:3; Prov. 10:19), or a close synonym that implies observation or comprehension or some act that leads to *wisdom*; correct comprehension brings wisdom, which in more recent versions has been translated "success" (Revised Standard Version, American Standard Version, New International Version). This meaning, however, is more derivative than primary. This

the New International Version translators admitted when
they placed the word *success* in 1 Samuel 18:14, in which
the King James Version gives a more accurate translation; "David behaved himself wisely in all his ways; and
the LORD was with him."

Biblical Prosperity

A word more closely allied to "success" is the Hebrew
word *tsaleach* (BDB:852), which is translated "prosper" or
"prosperity" fifty-two times in the KJV. Second Chronicles
26:5, concerning the reign of Uzziah, would be a typical
verse: "And he sought God in the days of Zechariah, who
had understanding in the visions of God: and as long as
he sought the LORD, God made him to prosper."

The word is also used in reference to war or battle.
Jeremiah prophesied against Zedekiah, king of Judah,
"Though ye fight with the Chaldeans, ye shall not prosper" (Jer. 32:5). Though the NIV has chosen to translate
the word *tsaleach* as "success" in the above and several
other instances, there is nothing to indicate from the context that the original word connotes anything other than
the quite limited meaning of tangible possessions, physical health, and military victory.

The NIV indicates concerning the imprisoned Joseph
that the Lord was with him "and gave him success
(*tsaleach*) in whatever he did" (Gen. 39:23). In other
words, whatever he attempted to do worked out, or had
favorable results. At this point, the Hebrew word is
roughly equivalent to the Latin *succedere,* "to follow
after"; that is, intended results are subsequent to plans.
It cannot be safely argued that the Hebrew meant
tsaleach as intrinsic reward, internal satisfaction, doing
one's best, or other connotations of the Anglo-Saxon word
success as it has developed in American terminology within the past fifty years. The root meaning is more simplistic, according to John Hartley: "to accomplish satisfactorily what is intended" (Harris 1980:766). This can even

apply to the wicked and their deceitful means (Jer. 12:1; Dan. 8:12).

Shalom

In 1 Chronicles 12:18, when the captain of David's army pronounces a blessing of peace upon David, the NIV chooses to substitute the word *success* for *peace*. This is a translation of *shalom,* the best-known Hebrew word to us. Actually, the word has a wider connotation than "tranquility, quietness, or reconciliation." It can also mean "welfare, soundness, completeness, and security," which indicate that a person is faring well mentally and spiritually as well as physically. *Shalom* (BDB:1022) has a richer connotation than the teleological assumption of the Latin word *succedere,* from which *succeed* is derived. *Shalom* is a more value-laden word than *success.* Unless means and ends are specifically defined, the word *success* does not contain an idea of value. *Shalom* has positive meaning in and of itself. The word *success* does not do the word *shalom* justice in translation, and quite often, *success* is defined exclusive of "peace."

At the very least, the above indicates that the translator of Scripture does not escape applying the cultural connotations of his or her day.

Equality of God's People

The word *success* is an industrial-age term that relates more to job status and production. An equivalent Hebrew or Greek word for *production* does not appear anywhere in Scripture. In an industrial, assembly-line economy, the mark of ultimate success is financial independence: not having to be in someone else's employ. In the early Hebrew economy there was nothing exceptional about working within an intradependent strata. Except for the tradesmen inside the walls of the city, the land was the source of wealth, and if a person did not own any land, he was likely a slave to the person or family who did. To be free was to live in a subsistent, self-contained clan, not enslaved to a universal monetary or mercantile system. No one gave out kudos to those who maintained their place in the system. God envisioned this kind of "clannish" economic independence as the norm for the Hebrew people and not the exception.

Egalitarianism was extremely important to God and his theocratic economy. That was the reason the Year of Jubilee was instituted (Lev. 25). No matter how deeply in debt a family found itself, or how much of the land it had "pawned" for collateral, there was the opportunity for a fresh start. Such a plan took the edge off both aristocracy through inheritance and wealth through upward mobility. Many of the principles of capitalistic success were either discouraged or outright forbidden in the Hebrew economy: usury, mega-accumulation of real estate, and enslaving indebtedness.

Success of the Priests and Prophets

The word *tsaleach,* translated "prosper," is never used in relation to the priests and prophets. They were prosperous only to the extent that the people were prosperous, which was most often defined in terms of *shalom,* particularly by the major prophets (Isa. 66:12). Over and over again we are led to believe that the peace they enjoyed resulted from the truth they spoke and implemented. Both priests and prophets were to be absolutely sure of God's instructions and then to perform or communicate them as carefully as possible. Extreme sensitivity to God's voice was the intrinsic nature of their responsibilities.

No preacher in the Old Testament is a more shining example of the above than Samuel, who wore the dual mantle of both prophet and priest. Samuel's question to Saul after he had been victorious (prosperous) in battle formulated a paramount standard for the office of king, prophet, and priest. "Does the LORD delight in burnt offerings and sacrifice as much as in obeying the voice of the LORD? To obey is better than sacrifice, and to heed is better than the fat of rams" (1 Sam. 15:22).

Obedience was the primary criterion in the Old Testament for pastoral success. If the priest or prophet deviated from this standard, or placed his own prosperity before that of the people, he was a hireling. A hireling was any "spiritual" leader whose chief motive was material gain. God had instituted a system whereby the material needs of the priests would be taken care of on a daily basis.

The *sakar* (BDB:969) was the part of the tabernacle sacrifice that was to go to the priests for their sustenance. Since there was sacrifice on a daily basis, there was provision on a daily basis. Thus the priests had no need to preserve food for long periods of time or lay up provision for the future.

The ownership of land was not to be the lot of the Levites (Num. 18:24). Hence they had little opportunity for economic upward mobility. Their very survival depended on the stewardship of the people to whom they ministered. Joshua was faithful to carry out the basic principle of spiritual leadership: "But to the tribe of Levi he gave no inheritance, since the offerings made by fire to the LORD, the God of Israel, are their inheritance, as he promised them" (Josh. 13:14).

Implicit in this arrangement was that the reward of the priests was to be spiritual and supernatural rather than material and empirical. It was left to the monastics and mystics throughout the history of the church to articulate this concept. They believed it to be impossible to own material possessions without the possessions owning them, at least to some extent, and thus separating them from God. They believed material and financial success was dangerous to spiritual prosperity, a view which seems to have had some foundation in the exhortations of Christ.

No single portion of Old Testament Scripture more clearly explicates the characteristics of a "successful" person than Psalm 1. Whatever benefits or blessings he accrues are clearly contingent on verses 1 and 2: "Blessed (*'esher*) is the man who does not walk in the counsel of the wicked or stand in the way of sinners or sit in the seat of mockers. But his delight is in the law of the LORD, and on his law he meditates day and night." The word *'esher* (BDB:80) connotes "happiness and contentment," meanings that can be contextually derived only when the word *success* is used. *Peace* and *blessedness* carry meanings about intrinsic values that the word *success* does not.

In summary, *success* is not as precise a word as several Hebrew words we have drawn attention to: *'esher* (blessed), *sakal* (wise), and *shalom* (peace). *Success* does not bear the rich meanings of these words, which are normally in the context of a relationship to Yahweh. A person may be successful without knowing God, that is, accomplish ends, but cannot be blessed, wise, or experience peace outside of Yahweh. In the Old Testament, if a person is blessed, his righteousness is assumed. Neither wickedness nor righteousness can be assumed in *success* unless there is indication in the context. Thus, in most instances, substituting the Anglo-Saxon word *success* lacks the precision of corresponding Hebrew terms.

Prosperity is a more inexact word than the above examples, and like *success* has to be contextually defined. Both the wicked and righteous prosper. Recent translator tendencies to substitute the word *success* for *prosperity* indicate the contemporaneousness of the word. But we need to keep in mind that *success* is a buzz word for an industrial, technological, upwardly mobile society. It contains implications of pull-yourself-up-by-your-own-bootstraps individualism, and many other images that are extraneous to the prosperity of the Mosaic economy. Such modern-day images of achievement and getting ahead of the pack imposed on a biblical culture are an anachronism.

New Testament Key Words

The Hebrew word "tsaleach" is translated "euodoo" in the Septuagint (Bauer, Arndt, and Gingrich [BAG] 1979:323). This word appears with far less frequency in the New Testament than it does in the Septuagint. Again, the word largely connotes physical and material blessing, such as in the instruction for a person to give according "as God hath prospered him" (1 Cor. 16:2), or the simple accomplishment of an intended end as in Romans 1:10 (another instance where the NIV and New American Standard Bible have chosen the word *succeed* rather than the KJV's *prosper*). *Euodoo* means literally "to be led along a good road" (Friedrich 1967:113) and is used only in the passive voice in the New Testament. There is no connotation in the word suggesting the success resulting from self-initiative or achievement.

The word *euporeo* (Septuagint, Lev. 25:26–49; BAG:324) and its derivatives are used less often than *euodoo* and in a more limited sense being strictly related to earnings or money, as in Acts 11:29, 19:25. The one exception to this is 3 John 2: "Dear friend, I pray that you may enjoy good health and that all may go well with you, even as your soul is getting along well." That John meant anything other than spiritual health in his prayer would be pure conjecture. It is true that we get the word psychology from the Greek word for soul, *psyche*, but it would be weak logic to assume that John had some kind of concern for the psychological state of his friend. In what are probably the two best-known verses concerning the mind in Scripture (Rom. 12:2 and 2 Tim. 1:7), Paul does not use the word *psyche*.

Before we look at actual New Testament models of pastoral success, there is one other New Testament word that warrants closer scrutiny, *euarestos* (BAG:318). This word is used exclusively to describe a vertical relationship, that which is "pleasing" and "acceptable" to God. Certainly Paul has the Old Testament sacrificial system in mind when he exhorts us to present our bodies "holy, acceptable unto him" (Rom. 12:1). The ultimate concern for everything a person does is that it pleases God. Whatever the product of our labors, it is crucial that they be pleasing to God. Paul stated that the criterion for assessing the practice of the church was that it would be acceptable to God (1 Tim. 5:4). This principle of evaluating performance by God's standards rather than humans' is as old as the story of Cain and Abel.

Christ and Professional Ministry

The first hint of Jesus' thoughts on the professional ministry comes in the Sermon on the Mount. Ostentation is a temptation of ministry. In Jesus' day it was a particular temptation to those who devoted extensive amounts of time and energy to religious acts. Fasting, giving, praying could be used to attract attention and enhance prestige. This reward of immediate self-gratification was the temptation Jesus warned against in Matthew 6:1–6.

Jesus went so far as to say that such displays of pious acts would negate the successes that were most critical: communion with God and answered prayer. "When you pray, go into your room, close the door and pray to your Father, who is unseen. Then your Father, who sees what is done in secret, will reward you" (Matt. 6:6). Foremost in Christ's ministry was to provide the model of a perfect relationship with his Father, a relationship to which he refers no less than 103 times in the Gospel of John. Handing out plaques, certificates, and other tangible signs of recognition did not seem to be too high on the Galilean's agenda.

The Eschatological Assessment of Ministry

There has been an ongoing debate as to how the Jewish people interpreted eschatology. It is beyond the scope of this investigation to unravel that theological question. Even in such spiritually oriented pronouncements as Proverbs 28:13, "He who conceals his sins does not prosper," there is not sufficient contextual evidence that the verse has eschatological ramifications. But we know that prosperity and righteousness are closely related. The blessing of God as so clearly articulated by Moses in the book of Deuteronomy was contingent on obedience to God's law, and not necessarily on entrepreneurship or clever financial planning.

Reward (*misthos,* BAG:523) recurs throughout the New Testament, appearing no less than thirteen times in Christ's most famous sermon. In the ministry and teachings of Jesus, *reward* (recompense or wages) takes on a decidedly eschatological connotation as in Matthew 5:12 and Luke 6:23. In fact, the context of these verses leads us to believe that the reward received in heaven will be inversely proportionate to the rewards enjoyed on earth. When Christ sent out the twelve for full-time ministry, he was clear about their wages. The itinerant evangelists could expect the necessities of life, shelter, clothing, and food, to be directly provided by those to whom they ministered. Since there would be no need to buy these items, there was no need for them to carry gold or silver (Matt. 10:9, 10). Besides basic provisions, the disciples could expect rejection (v. 14), betrayal (v. 17), physical abuse (v. 17), hatred (v. 22), and ultimately, martyrdom. (These are not the fringe benefits for which most pastors are clamoring.)

God's omnipresent sovereignty would go with his ambassadors, and his providence would undergird them into the next life. Those overly concerned with their fortunes in this life, such as physical well-being and family serenity, were in danger of losing everything in the end (Matt. 10:39). Not only was an eternal reward promised to a "cross-bearing" ministry but also to those who identify with such a ministry: "Anyone who receives a prophet because he is a prophet will receive a prophet's reward, and anyone who receives a righteous man because he is a righteous man will receive a righteous man's reward" (Matt. 10:41).

No words of Jesus are more explicit concerning the eschatological reward of ministry than when he first announced to his disciples that he himself must go to Jerusalem for crucifixion. Finding, offering, and overvaluing the life of flesh and time would mean forfeiture in the next (Matt. 16:24–26). As to final assessment of success, it would be left to God (it has a ring of finality and infallibility). "For the Son of Man is going to come in his Father's glory with his angels, and then he will reward each person according to what he has done" (v. 27).

There are two things obvious concerning Christ's ultimate and infinite appraisal of people's finite activities. First, as humans we have such difficulty in recognizing that which is of true value that it is sometimes futile to appraise what is done in this life. Christ will make the final assessment. Secondly, one might begin to suspect that the better things are going here, the worse they may turn out in the hereafter. When ministry is going well there is an even greater need for the pastor to check his eschatological bearings. Jesus tersely replied to the dynamic and sensational success of the disciples: "However, do not rejoice that the spirits submit to you, but rejoice that your names are written in heaven" (Luke 10:20).

An overt teaching of Christ was that the eschatological assessment of ministry is more important than any kind of temporal, quantifiable, or measurable assessment. It is this very principle that renders Christian ministry unique among all other activities. Everything done by the pastor has an eschatological ramification: it can be assessed only from the perception of eternity. What measures great here may be measured small there. The widow's mite tallied small on the treasurer's ledger, but it was a sacrifice worthy of unusual proclamation in God's

estimation. It is only in the "eschaton" that God will recognize and make known the true worth of everything
done in the flesh. Thomas Oden well states the uniqueness of Christian ministry within the eternal framework:

> One major difference between the church and other volun-
> tary or business or governmental organizations hinges on
> Christianity's eschatological perspective. Voluntary and
> business organizations generally have hedonic goals. They
> wish to accomplish objectives that are visible within this
> temporal sphere, often those that fit within a five-year
> plan, a fiscal year, or a three-week sales blitz. The church
> also has a bottom line at the end of the fiscal year, but
> that is not the only way it assesses itself. Christian con-
> gregations also try to get things done, organize things
> decently, and achieve objectives, but the Christian com-
> munity has a larger historical perspective on all of these
> activities—larger in fact than this fiscal year, this political
> regime, or even this civilization (Oden 1983:162).

Neither Thomas Oden nor I mean to say that all activities, whether "secular" or "spiritual" do not have eschatological ramifications.

Eschatology places the matters of this life within the
perspective of quality rather than quantity. No analogy in
Jesus' teachings shows this more beautifully than that of
the wedding. The church is to prepare a bride for the
bridegroom. Not only the bride but also the entire wedding party is to be properly attired. In Jesus' Middle
Eastern culture, how the wedding party was dressed was
more significant than how many guests were present.
Proper dress meant unity and allegiance to the king. In
the Matthew 22 parable, someone had invited a guest
but had failed to advise him that mere attendance at the
event was insufficient to signify faithfulness. A bride
properly attired and prepared for the Lamb, ready to
stand before him in her wedding garment, is the ultimate goal of ministry. Anything short of that is absolute
failure.

Inclusiveness of Biblical Ministry

The story of the wedding feast in Matthew 22:1–14 points us to another critical focus of Christ's ministry. Those who are outcasts, impoverished, physically diseased, or deformed have a special place in his concern. Christ indicated this when he responded to the disciples of John the Baptist questioning his true identity. To validate that he was the sent one, that his credentials were in order, Jesus sent the following back to John:

Vita: Jesus the Christ
Blind receive sight
Lame walk
Lepers cured
Deaf hear
Dead raised
Good news preached to the poor (Matt. 11:4–6)

It was this identification with the outcasts that authenticated the ministry of Christ. The members of his board were not exactly the cream of the crop. In no one was the common man—the "whosoeverness" of the gospel—more typified than in John the Baptist. In the Matthew 11 passage, Christ authenticated the ministry of John not only by labeling him great, but designating him as a minister for all time.

Vita: John the Baptist
Resides in the desert
Not easily swayed
Rough-hewn
Coarse clothes
Proclaims Christ
Aggressive
Speaks truth (Matt. 11:7–10)

The Leveling of Grace

But it is also in this passage that Christ gives his most explicit criterion for greatness, a criterion that overshadows certifiable achievement: "Yet he who is least in the kingdom of heaven is greater than he [John the Baptist]" (Matt. 11:11). Does the next verse give us insight into this parenthetical observation of Christ? "From the days of John the Baptist until now, the kingdom of heaven has been forcefully advancing, and forceful men lay hold of it" (Matt. 11:12). No matter how much a person accomplishes, no matter how aggressive a person is, he or she does not measure up to the person who has experienced grace, grace received into a childlike, humble, and trustful heart. Christ juxtaposes the radicalism of grace with the philosophy of self-reliance, achievement, and the rewards of hard work. In the parable of the wage earners, those who had slaved all day in the hot sun were paid no more than those who had worked only an hour in the cool of the day (Matt. 20:1–16).

Jesus never hesitated to say who is greatest. Only those with childlike, nonassuming, self-sacrificial attitudes meet the stipulations of ministry. It was difficult for the disciples to grasp. It was the paradox that Jesus attempted to illustrate by way of an object lesson in his last hours with them—the last course of their "seminary training." Only the most advanced, spiritually mature could grasp it. "But many who are first will be last, and many who are last will be first" (Matt. 19:30). Not even the forsaking of parents, riches, inheritance, and comfort would guarantee greatness. Radical grace was spelled out by Christ in what someone has called a theology of reversal. It was a theology incompatible with the culture of Christ's and of every society before or since. Ours is certainly no exception. John Francis Kavanaugh writes:

> Christ reveals that human fulfillment is found in the opposite of riches (whether spiritual or, as Luke more

directly says, material), the opposite of mere good times and absence of suffering, the opposite of being powerful, unforgiving, the opposite of war making, even the opposite of victory. Nietzsche found this doctrine scandalous, and attacked it as the demeaning of the will to power (Kavanaugh 1981:72).

Grace versus Psychological Fulfillment

It is the above truth that makes ministry precarious. There is no profession that offers more potential for positive strokes and kudos. The pastor's intimacy with a congregation offers more acceptance and psychological feedback in a year than many other occupations offer in a lifetime. Residents of a city of fifty thousand or fewer can more readily tell you which pastor in town is most successful than they can which attorney or which medical doctor.

A deep psychological need to be recognized, loved, and accepted can be an unconscious motive for ministry. But obsession with such gratifications can also be the very thing that destroys the effectiveness of ministry. For that reason, the classic literature on ministry cautions those who are overly eager to enter the profession. Richard Baxter duly warned against wrong motives that were self-serving while they eliminated self-denial. Gregory the Great clearly articulated the precarious psychological balance the pastor needs to maintain:

> He then, who is over others ought to study to be loved to the end that he may be listened to, and shall not seek love for its own sake, lest he be found in the hidden usurpation of his thought to rebel against Him whom in his office he appears to serve (Gregory the Great *Nicene Fathers,* 1956:20).

Gregory the Great's comments on the motives and objectives of pastoral care have hardly been surpassed, but they have been updated with fresh psychological insight. Jacob Firet cites the following psychological needs of ministers: "the need for accomplishment, the need for aggression, the need to dominate, the need for attaching oneself to others, the need to make an impression, the need to be seen and heard, the need to support, to comfort, to take 'care of'" (Firet 1986:242). Firet goes on to illustrate how a wrong motive can be debilitating:

> But when, for example, the desire to help others in their troubles is coupled with the desire to dominate, or the desire to gain insight into complex matters is interwoven with the desire to shine in the eyes of others, the danger exists to say the least, that the entire role-performance of the pastor is pervasively affected by an air of non-objectivity and artificiality (Firet 1986:243).

It was Christ who first raised the red flag. "Woe to you when all speak well of you, for that is how their fathers treated the false prophets" (Luke 6:26). Universal applause rather than lack of it is cause for alarm. Except for those few movie stars and athletes who are household names, the pastor can more easily become a household name in at least four or five hundred homes than a person in any other profession. A typical pastor, at least one who is not at great odds with his congregation, will receive more commendation after one Sunday morning message than most people receive in a year. Dependence on such horizontal affirmation rather than the "inner witness of the Spirit" is one of the greatest hazards of ministry. It is a primary reason some preachers experience psychological swings. Instant gratification is fickle and fleeting and leads to the Monday morning blues. Henry Ward Beecher, who confessed that there was "nothing in this world that is such a stimulus to me as an audience" (Hibben 1942:295), wrote:

> A minister says: "I am very sensitive to the praise and opinions of men. When I speak, I can't get rid of the feeling of myself. I am standing before a thousand people, and

I am all the time thinking about myself." . . . What is
such a man to do? Can he change his own temperament?
. . . How can a man alter the laws that are laid down for
him? (Hibben 1942:254).

A Simple Scriptural Formula for Success

No single passage of Scripture combines eschatology,
obscurity, and ministry to those in need more effectively
than Matthew 25:31–46. And no other portion of
Scripture so unequivocally connects particular deeds with
a particular reward. The formula seems almost too simple to be true. Those who fed the hungry, clothed the
naked, visited the sick, and did so without fanfare in a
nonpresumptive manner, heard "Come, you who are
blessed by my Father, take your inheritance, the kingdom
prepared for you since the creation of the world" (Matt.
25:34). Ignatius of Loyola in his *Spiritual Exercise* said
regarding his love for the poor, "I will consider that I am
at the Day of Judgement and I will reflect on how I
should then wish to have fulfilled the duties of my ministry" (Oden 1986:149).

What is most striking about the above Matthew passage is its perspective of the commonality and the simplicity of the commonality. Persons are eternally designated as sheep or goats on the basis of whether or not
they were sensitive to the external needs that have exist-
ed in all societies at all times in varying degrees. It was
this portion of Scripture that deeply impressed John and
Charles Wesley as well as the others who met for mutual
soul-searching in the "Holy Club" while they were Oxford
students. After beginning to visit the local prisons
because they thought it their bounden duty, they were
scoffed at by fellow students. In bewilderment, John
wrote home to his father, questioning the propriety of
their ministry. Samuel tersely responded in the following
words: "I question whether a mortal can arrive to a
greater degree of perfection than steadily to do good, and

for that very reason patiently and meekly to suffer evil. Bear no more sail than is necessary, but steer steady" (Telford 1953:62).

Valid ministry has always been marked by unostentatious care of the disadvantaged. The following from the pen of John Wesley profoundly states its simple eschatological formula: "It is true that I travel 5000 miles a year to visit the poor. I must do so if I believe the gospel. I must do so if I believe that is the standard by which the great shepherd in that last day will judge his sheep." Because of the above, Richard Niebuhr said the English Methodist revival was the last great religious revolution among the disinherited.

Faithfulness

The final principle of pastoral success we will note comes from the same teaching of Christ. It, too, has eschatological implications. The stewards in the parable of the talents were rewarded for their faithfulness. Those who had done the best they could with what they had were told, "Well done, good and faithful servant! You have been faithful with a few things; I will put you in charge of many things. Come and share your master's happiness" (Matt. 25:21)! He who had earned two talents received the same as he who had earned five talents. Success was defined as realization of potentiality. In this sense, success is extremely relative: "to . . . each according to his ability" (Matt. 25:15). Literally translated, this passage means "according to individual ability." *Idou* means "belonging to an individual" (BAG:370). The standards for success are as unique and varied as are individual persons.

Any kind of objective, measurable, absolute standard is, at least in this life, both futile and false. Comparisons made according to a standard measure of achievement miss this crucial teaching of Christ. The central motif of Matthew 25 is that God has entrusted to each individual unique abilities—gifts, talents—but that person is successful only as far as he meets his unique, God-given opportunities to use those abilities. Thus it is theoretically possible to have attained a visibly high degree of measurable achievement and at the same time be very unsuccessful in God's eyes, as this maxim says: Most of us ask for opportunities equal to our abilities rather than abilities equal to our opportunities. But the Christian's prayer for success is "Lord, help me to meet the opportunities that are mine today." The pastor's prayer should be no different. Willingness is more important than ability. God will see to it that we have all of the latter that we are willing to utilize for his glory. Alexander MacLaren tersely reminds us:

> Our aim rather than our capacity determines our character, and they who greatly aspire after the greatest things within the reach of men, which are faith, hope, charity and who for the sake of effecting those aspirations, put their heels upon the head of the serpent and suppress the animal in their nature, these are the men "great in the sight of the Lord" (MacLaren 1902:241).

Stewardship of opportunities has to be defined before success can be appraised. Every pastor's opportunities are unique to him and his parish. Moment-by-moment alertness to God in the midst of opportunities is his proper motivation and agenda. Comparing his church's statistics with those of others can be self-defeating, depressing, devastating. Maintaining a spiritual checklist between himself and God is the pastor's ultimate measure of worth.

Enos Martin addresses the common, highly competitive attitude in pastors:

> In subtle ways they frequently check on how they compare with neighboring ministers. If they feel superior to others, it helps quiet the nagging inner voice that they are inferior. This conflict between the idealized self and the

actual self is often manifested as an "all or none" attitude
in pastors. Either they are "all perfect" with no failures, or
they are "nothing" (Martin 1982:83).

Martin touches on a critical issue. There is no such
thing as either/or success in ministry, only degrees of success. Would not Jesus have had the right to ask the earn-
er of the five talents why he had not invested it in a different stock so he could have received an even greater
yield? We would grant to the successful investor business
acumen in the investment, but every investor knows that
there are no guarantees. If that be the nature of securities brokering, the fact is multiplied a thousand times in
ministry.

In a very enlightening article in *Leadership*, C. Peter
Wagner, the dean of church-growth analysts, was posed
this question: How about a church whose membership
declined from 2000 in 1960 to 800 members in 1970, and
then to 400 in 1980 due to rapid demographic changes in
the surrounding community? . . . Would you call that a
successful church (*Leadership* 1981:129)? Before giving
Wagner's answer, we need to acknowledge that he does
believe there are churches with "ethnikitis" (Wagner's
neologism), a sociological and demographic disease the
church can do little or nothing to rectify. Its main cause is
the rapidly changing communities that surround a
church. Wagner also believes there are pastors who are
called by God to lead numerically nongrowing churches.

Now, to the above question Wagner answered,
"Borderline" (*Leadership* 1981:129)! It seems to me that
an unqualified "borderline" misses the point of obedience
and faithfulness. Might not the church that takes particular remedies to foster growth, such as reaching beyond
the community for its own clientele or simply leaving the
community, be less successful than a church that, though
it is fully aware of the long-term ramifications, continues
to minister after the manner of Christ? Which people
need pastoral care more than those whose factories have

been shut down or whose farms have been repossessed or who have been disfellowshiped because they have moved to a new community?

Yet to remain in such a community would mean crucifixion—numerically and ecclesiastically. "It's a dead-end street." That's what Peter told Jesus when the latter unveiled his plans to go to Jerusalem for some pastoral purposes (Matt. 16:21). Peter in effect warned him it would be the end of his career (v. 22). Peter's rationale was so plausible, feasible, and subtle that Christ reacted more vehemently than he had ever responded to any individual, much less a friend: "Out of my sight, Satan" (v. 23)! The temptation was so great that it demanded a radical response.

The temptation to deviate from God's purposes for ministry also is so overwhelming, to stay on course demands radical obedience. Such steadfastness will not be understood by very many people. In fact, Christ was so misunderstood that they killed him. Men killed God—the most outstanding and despicable act in the history of mankind. But out of that despicable act comes every meaningful act of redemptive ministry that was ever rendered.

Conclusion

There are biblical standards for success in ministry. The danger is that we impose contemporary principles of success on them and fail to encourage today's pastors to emulate the New Testament models. Everything done in the church needs to be examined and evaluated through a christological lens. The lens magnifies Christ and minimizes self, which helps to keep all achievement in proper perspective. At the apex of the cross all production must pass inspection. As Oswald Chambers reminds us, "Sum up the life of Jesus Christ by any other standard than God's, and it is an anticlimax of failure. 'It is required in stewards, that a man be found faithful'—not successful" (Chambers 1987:342).

7

A Pauline Doctrine
of Success

Lord Jesus, I come to thee for spiritual preparation. Lay thy hand upon me. Anoint me with the oil of the New Testament prophet. Forbid that I should become a religious scribe and thus lose my prophetic calling. Save me from the curse that lies dark across the face of the modern clergy, the curse of compromise, of imitation, of professionalism. Save me from the error of judging a church by its size, its popularity or the amount of its yearly offering. Help me to remember that I am a prophet, not a promoter, not a religious manager but a prophet. . . . Let me never become a slave to crowds.
A. W. Tozer

In the Book of Acts, chapters 13–27, we have described for us the ministerial career of Paul of Tarsus. For approximately thirty years, Paul served Christ in the capacities of both evangelist and pastor. Though he stopped in scores of places, many of them repeatedly, the Bible tells us exactly what he did and what were the results of his activities in only twenty-five of those visits. Viewed pragmatically, as through the eyes of a "Board of Ministry," his career would appear to be quite checkered. In nine of the places where Paul stopped he was beaten, stoned, or jailed, resulting in his fleeing for his life or leaving out of disgust. To say there was a cloud over his departures would be an understatement. On a form I recently filled out for transferring my ministerial credentials from one denomination to another, I was asked, "Have you had trouble in any of your churches?" Based on that criterion the denomination would have turned down Paul's application.

If moderation is the rule of life for the professional *homo religioso,* Paul never enjoyed it. There always seemed to be either too much emotion or not enough of it. At least three times his preaching started riots, but on another occasion his sermon was so long and dull that a man went to sleep, fell out of his seat, and was killed. On yet another occasion, Paul was so successful that he was worshiped as a god. In only seven instances does Paul's biographer tell us that Paul's revivalistic effort gained great numbers of converts (Acts 14:1; 14:21; 16:5; 17:4; 17:12; 18:8; 19:18). Striking fire only seven times over a lifetime of evangelistic effort will certainly diminish an evangelist's reputation. The phone will ring less and less frequently from faraway cities, and the inviting churches will be increasingly smaller. As Donald Guthrie has summarized, "On many of the occasions in Acts his so-called eloquence was far from persuasive, for it frequently resulted in open hostility and on at least one occasion in ridicule" (Guthrie 1970:358).

Just plain "bad luck" seemed to dog Paul wherever he went. Hear him tell it in his own words:

> Five times I received from the Jews the forty lashes minus one. Three times I was beaten with rods, once I was stoned, three times I was shipwrecked, I spent a night and a day in the open sea, I have been constantly on the move. I have been in danger from rivers, in danger from bandits, in danger from my own countrymen, in danger from Gentiles; in danger in the city, in danger in the country, in danger at sea; and in danger from false brothers. I have labored and toiled and have often gone without sleep; I have known hunger and thirst and have often

gone without food; I have been cold and naked (2 Cor. 11:24–27).

Is Paul making a case for early retirement? Is he second-guessing his life's vocation? Is he experiencing burnout or a midlife crisis? If you answered yes to any of the above, you are wrong. What Paul is doing is validating his apostleship. The formula goes something like this: the more a person suffers, the more likely it is that he or she is called of God. But this is not to say that all suffering is cross-bearing. There is something reassuring to the apostle concerning a ministry which is "in spite of rather than because of" suffering. "If I must boast, I will boast of the things that show my weakness" (2 Cor. 11:30). Paul is saying, "In spite of physical infirmity, in spite of deficiency in speech, in spite of an unattractive appearance, God has used me for his glory. It is these very weaknesses and negative circumstances that allow me to be successful, because his power is made perfect in my weakness." He writes, "But we have this treasure in jars of clay to show that this all-surpassing power is from God and not from us" (2 Cor. 4:7).

At no point in his life did Paul point to statistical results of his labor to authenticate his success; X number of churches planted, X number of converts won, plus X number of books written, plus X number of offices held, plus X number of boards served on were not a part of his success formula. But Paul was very concerned about results and the ability to substantiate them from a rational and spiritual perspective. While it is much easier to count converts than evaluate quality of ministry, Paul's writings concerning his converts emphasize his producing in them qualities of character rather than his converts producing converts.

Paul's Apology of Ministry

The case in point that is worth a careful look is Paul's parting message to the Ephesian elders, found in Acts

20. F. F. Bruce reminds us that it is the only Pauline speech delivered to Christians that Luke has recorded (Bruce 1977:412). Paul reviews his years of ministry to that congregation. He said the validity of his bona fide labors consisted of the following:

Humility

Verse 19. Although Paul's ministry was characterized by humility, it was not a "poor me, woe is me" kind of humility. In fact, Paul was not too inhibited to exhort believers to follow his example (Phil. 3:17). Humility for Paul meant that he was content with the lot God had given him and above all he was not dependent on his own abilities. He had a confidence and security that rested in God's strength.

Humility is a frame of reference that perceives all of life as a gift from a sovereign and gracious God. The "ego" is a channel between God's enablement and life's needs. Bruce states: "It was a naturally proud man who schooled himself to boast about his humiliation in place of his achievements" (Bruce 1977:460).

Empathy

Verse 19. Paul was empathetic to the point of tears. However, Paul's tears did not demonstrate only a sentimental and emotional concern. His caring was in a sacrificial mode that identified with the hurts of others. He understood the importance of perceiving the hurts and despair of others from their perspective. William Booth was asked the secret to evangelism and he tersely responded, "Try tears."

Faithful Teaching

Verse 20. Paul faithfully preached and taught, both publicly and privately. Presenting the *kerygma* to believers was critical to the welfare of the church. The person who did not promote teaching truth, catechism, doctrine, was opening the doors for the wolves of heresy (vv. 29–30).

When Paul wrote to the young pastor Timothy, he made the aptitude for teaching a high criterion for success (1 Tim. 3:2; 2 Tim. 2:24).

It may be that Paul believed teaching (*didache* [doctrine]) to be his very highest duty. It is the only duty he wraps in an eschatological context. It is the responsibility he most emphatically declares as the full discharge of his duty. "Therefore, I declare to you today that I am innocent of the blood of all men. For I have not hesitated to proclaim to you the whole will of God" (vv. 26–27). Paul is saying that if I have failed to preach a full-orbed gospel, I am guilty of shirking my primary obligation. Faith is based on reason, and correct reason is based on correct information. Maturity of faith grows on maturity of knowledge, a knowledge that is more than simply accumulation of facts and is also the quest for the full-orbed truth found in Jesus Christ.

As a young pastor surrounded by upper-middle class parishioners, I was severely criticized for my preaching by a certain group of people (parishioners' criticism about sermonizing is rarely completely unjustified). The point of most of the criticism concerned a theology in vogue at that time, and my parishioners, from their perspective, were not hearing enough of it. As I was taking the well-known pastor/evangelist Dr. Paul Rees to the airport one morning, I asked him about the particular criticism I was enduring. He quickly reminded me of Acts 20:27, preaching "all the counsel of God" (KJV).

The preacher must not harbor pet doctrines or proclaim faddish theologies. He will have to preach God's holiness, justice, and wrath as well as his love and mercy. Paul himself said it best, "Note then the severity and mercy of God" (Rom. 11:22). The hearers' repentance and restitution will need to be addressed as readily as their self-worth and fulfillment. Paul was echoing the solemn warning of Ezekiel that he whose teaching does not include admonition to the unrighteous will be accountable for the blood of those who do not repent (Ezek. 33:8).

The early church adapted the word *catechism* from the less frequently used New Testament Greek word for teaching, *katexio*. This word connotes the systematic teaching of a given subject. Etymologically, *catechism* became known as instruction specifically in religious knowledge. Paul sensed this teaching responsibility as more than simply a defensive posture. Going from "house to house" for catechism was not stated in Paul's job description by a pastor-parish relations committee; it was something that he took the initiative to carry out. The tremendous consumption of time and energy the task of catechizing deserves is described by Richard Baxter:

> We spend Mondays and Tuesdays, from morning to about nightfall, in the work . . . taking about fifteen or sixteen families in a week, that we may go through the parish, which hath above eight hundred families, in a year: and I cannot say yet that one family have refused to come to me; and but few have excused themselves, and shifted it off: and I find more outward signs of success with most that come than of all my public preaching to them. . . . I take a catalogue of all the persons of understanding in the parish; and the clerk goes a week before to every family, to tell them when to come and at what hour. . . . I am forced, by the number, to deal with a whole family at once; but do not usually admit any of another family to be present (Baxter:29).

Universal Gospel

Verse 21: "I have declared to both Jews and Greeks that they must turn to God in repentance and have faith in our Lord Jesus." Paul was indiscriminate in preaching the gospel. He had proclaimed without fear or favor. Paul was not naive concerning the temptation to cater to particular kinds of people. It was he who so valiantly proclaimed (though just what he meant by this has been the subject of much debate): "To the weak I became weak, to win the weak. I have become all things to all men so that by all possible means I might save some" (1 Cor. 9:22).

Paul was not worried about being labeled paternalistic or condescending. His overriding passion was to reach people no matter what their plane of existence. In fact, Paul explicitly exhorts, "Do not be proud, but be willing to associate with people of low position" (Rom. 12:16).

Pastors and churches who have realized their calling have resisted favoritism, in spite of possible detriments to budget or prestige. Ambrose sold the holy vessels to redeem prisoners, stating, "Is it not much better that the priests should melt it down for the sustenance of the poor" (Oden 1986:146). The story is well known of St. Francis, who gave not only money but a kiss to a leper (Oden 1986:161). No literature of the church is more explicit about the care of the poor than the following from the *Constitutions of the Holy Apostles,* second century:

> Be solicitous about their maintenance, in nothing wanting to them; exhibiting to the orphans the care of parents; to the widows the care of husbands; to those of suitable age, marriage; to the artificer, work; to the unable, commiseration; to the strangers, an house; to the hungry, food; to the thirsty, drink; to the naked, clothing; to the sick, visitation; to the prisoners, assistance (*Constitution of the Holy Apostles* 1913:433).

Spirit Led

Verse 22. Paul exemplified obedience to the Holy Spirit in that he was "compelled by the Spirit." The original language has the idea of being given up to or yielded to the Holy Spirit. The text not only refers to the impetus or call of the Holy Spirit but also gives us clear insight into Paul's *modus operandi*. There was continuous communication between Paul and the Holy Spirit. The most vivid example of this was the direct message he received from God concerning his Macedonian ministry (Acts 16:6–10). That the missionary journeys of Paul received their commission and direction from the Holy Spirit was the interpretation of the historian Luke (Acts 13:4). Not only did

Paul receive direction to certain places but he was also restrained from going to others (Acts 16:6). His entire missionary career was done without demographies, statistical surveys, or census information. It was carried out under the power and by the direction of the Holy Spirit. This is not to say that he did not have a plan or strategy; rather, it was God's plan and God's strategy. Jacob Firet says, "The Spirit does not make conscious and planned action superfluous, he makes it possible" (Firet 1986:279).

Corporate planners call the above intuition, as opposed to rationalism. Peters and Waterman in their best seller, *In Search of Excellence,* point out that most successful companies rely more on intuitive innovation, gut feeling, and common sense, than on an overly rationalistic model based on scientific measurement. Going with a hunch is more important than reducing all odds to the lowest possibility of failure. Intestinal fortitude is more critical than informational fortitude. Peters and Waterman state, "An important finding from the excellent companies is the degree to which formal, rational sorting devices are bypassed" (Peters and Waterman 1982:216).

It seems ironic that naturalistic industry would argue for heart, while the supernaturalistic church of God is, at times, relying more on intellect. But we should not be surprised; there has been a history of rationalism throughout the centuries of the church. The church and its schools for training are increasingly turning to management skills and societal data for artillery. This involves the scientific analysis of both what evangelicals have to do well and to whom they sell it. There is a heavy reliance on the disciplines of anthropology, sociology, psychology, and in particular, marketing. Again, James Hunter reminds us of the present-day shift to the rationalization of Christianity, "the increased tendency toward systematization, codification, and methodization" (Hunter 1983:83).

Donald Guthrie says, "In spite of attempts to describe Paul's experience in psychological terms, there is something mysterious and miraculous about it which defies analysis" (Guthrie 1970:386–87). Analysis of results is more befitting accountants and engineers than it is holy men. Preparing attorneys and physicians is a categorically different task from that of preparing ministers. The former may confidently leave graduate school knowing that if they apply the tools they have been given in the way that they have been taught, they will be successful. A shepherd must not only graduate with shepherding skills but possess a willingness to lay down his life for the sheep. Such willingness comes not from academia but from supernatural empowerment.

"Defying analysis" was the experience of a group of students who went to interview a pastor whose worship service has almost five thousand people on Sunday morning. They expected to hear a list of how-to's and an emphasis on the importance of setting goals. Instead, the pastor criticized the overly bureaucratic organization of most churches and stressed the fact that his church had not planned ahead for any phase of its growth. It had just happened. His underlying theme was the importance of minimizing results while living in constant communication with God.

Such dependence on the Holy Spirit for ministry accents the truth that success is as vitally related to means as it is to ends. In fact, here may be the chief distinction between the church and the world. The world defines the means by the ends or goals pursued. The church defines its ends or goals by the means. Christ instructed his pastors first to take care of the means, and the goals would automatically take care of themselves. "Tarry . . . until ye be endued with power" (Luke 24:49 KJV), and "ye shall be witnesses unto me" (Acts 1:8 KJV). When the apostles were filled with the Holy Spirit, the church exploded, so to speak, over the face of the earth. As someone has succinctly said, "Church growth in the New Testament was not a goal, it was a result."

Reliance on the supernatural is a main ingredient of

successful ministry. It is no accident that in 1986 one denomination could boast having the single fastest-growing church in thirty-one of the fifty states. The Assemblies of God continue to stress the supernatural in their worship and preaching while simultaneously moderating the more frenzied fringes that have been historically a part of their profile. This emphasis appeals to middle-class people who are not searching for something weird but at the same time hunger for something or someone to lift them above the mundane drudgery of their everyday existence (no matter how glossy it may appear on the surface). Americans will increasingly turn to the supernatural as the glow of materialism fades.

One may rightly argue that juxtaposing Paul's mystical philosophy of ministry with the methods of the church in a telemarketing/mass-communication age is anachronistic. Who is to say that Paul would not have had his own personal computer? But does the church need to be reminded that the mystery of godliness is found in the paradoxes of the cross and not in the cold calculations of pure objectivity? Romantic spontaneity is the law of religion, rather than reaching the lowest common denominator of expenditure and risk. Falling in love is not a simple equation of energy plus time equals results. Preparing a bride is more a spiritual process than an academic one. That is the reason that Paul spent time alone with God in the Arabian desert after his conversion. Even though technical training may be important, the essentials of ministry come for the most part from the heart of God, not from institutions, textbooks, or even mentors.

Paul's Assessment of Results

Does the lack of statistical analysis in Paul's Ephesian address mean that he was totally oblivious to the results of his ministry? Hardly. We notice in Acts 13 that he followed Jesus' exhortation and shook the dust off his feet when the gospel was rejected. He stayed longer when his ministry was fruitful. The Bible gives us a vivid contrast between the response of the Bereans and the Thessalonians. Paul won a large number of disciples at Derbe (Acts 14), and many at Corinth believed and were baptized. Paul did not believe he was called to act in a vacuum without any assessment of the ramifications of his deeds. But the ramifications were more eternal than temporal. As Bruce says, "Above all, he hopes that when he gives a final account of his apostolic stewardship to the Lord who commissioned him, he will need to do no more than point to his converts and have the quality of his service judged by their faith and life" (Bruce 1977:459).

The answerable-only-ultimately-to-God principle is postulated in J. I. Packer's argument for the sovereignty of God in evangelism. He focuses on the incongruities of rationalistic speculation and systematic calculations with the demands of Scripture and the mystery of godliness. He cautions against the calculating approach that regards our job as not simply presenting Christ but actually producing converts. Packer writes:

> God saves in His own time and we ought not to suppose that He is in such as hurry as we are. We need to remember that we are all children of our age and the spirit of our age is a spirit of hurry. And it is a pragmatic spirit; it is a spirit that demands quick results. The modern ideal is to achieve more and more by doing less and less (Packer 1961:119).

However, I believe that James Packer's definition of evangelism is defective, or perhaps it simply falls short of the gospel mandate. He says, "According to the New Testament, evangelism is just preaching the gospel, the evangel. It is a work of communication in which Christians make themselves mouthpieces for God's message of mercy to sinners" (Packer 1961:41). It may be that the author is assuming something that I do not. Even when I am at my best, with the purest of intentions, I am not sure that what comes out of my mouth is exactly from

the Lord. I am willing to admit that my subjective interpretation may stand between my perception of the situation I confront and the reality of it. I am not sure that
simply to be a "mouthpiece" for God apart from subjective
perception and intellectual limitations is always within
the divine plan.

Paul stated in his letter to the Romans that he made
much of his ministry "in the hope that I may somehow
arouse my own people to envy and save some of them"
(Rom. 11:14). Arousing to envy is certainly a means. At
another point Paul urged for all possible means in saving
some (1 Cor. 9:22). Means can never be defined apart
from consequences and goals, and if Paul is arguing for a
consideration of means he is arguing for a consideration
of goals.

Thus a slight amendment is needed to Dr. Packer's definition: according to the New Testament, evangelism is
preaching the gospel *with a view to persons being saved*.
It is a work of communication in which Christians, as
much as lies within their ability under the power of the
Holy Spirit, make themselves mouthpieces for God's message of mercy to sinners. We need not eliminate means
and goals, only illegitimate means and goals. I must
purge goals that are out of wrong motives, means that are
insensitive, and methodologies that are more for my own
fulfillment than someone else's full potential in Christ.
Packer is fully aware of our need to tread cautiously:

> It must never be forgotten that the enterprise required of
> us in evangelism is the enterprise of love, an enterprise
> that springs from a genuine interest in those whom we
> seek to win, and genuine care for their well-being, and
> expresses itself in a genuine respect for them and a gen-
> uine friendliness toward them (Packer 1961:79–80).

Since means cannot be completely defined without reference to ends, it is simplistic to insist that evangelism be
defined solely in terms of its message, not its targets or
its results or the methods used. Artillery cannot be prop-

erly chosen with complete disregard for the target. Paul's target was to plant churches that resulted in success. Obedience to the Holy Spirit enabled him to plant at least fifteen churches in a lifetime of ministry. For a fuller discussion of whether or not the definition of evangelism should stress results, see *Evangelize! A Historical Survey of the Concept,* by David B. Barrett. There has been much disagreement on the subject.

Paul's Doctrine of Boasting

Because the matter of evaluating ministry was and is so delicate, there is a Pauline doctrine of boasting. Paul uses the word *boast* over twenty times in his writings. He was not naive concerning his contribution to the cause of the kingdom. No doubt sharing his triumphs with the church leadership while at the same time keeping them in proper perspective was a tension for Paul. He was naturally zealous, and tendencies to self-reliance were not eliminated on the Damascus road. How does one excel and at the same time be a passive instrument in the hands of God? Terrance Callan analyzes Paul's working through this particular conflict:

> Paul . . . boasts not only in God who acts through the surprising weakness of the cross and chooses the weak but also in his own weakness in which God is present and active. This turns upside down the ordinary idea of boasting, including Paul's own earlier understanding of boasting in the Lord. Now boasting is not a presentation of success, not even success as a servant of God, but of failure in which God's success is somehow to be found (Callan:47).

Paul's View of Spiritual Achievement

We must keep in mind that being concerned about producing and being certain about the validity of results are two different things. There is a vast difference between assessing the results of church growth and the quarterly profits of General Motors. Maturity in Christ is not easily calculable. In one sense, spiritual achievement is a contradiction in terms. The church-growth school readily admits this. But Paul adds even another dimension to the complexity of calculating success. "If any man builds on this foundation using gold, silver, costly stones, wood, hay or straw, his work will be shown for what it is, because the day will bring it to light. It will be revealed with fire, and the fire will test the quality of each man's work" (1 Cor. 3:12, 13).

By looking at the first part of this chapter we will gain a clear picture of what Paul meant by the above verses. His comments were aimed at those who were bragging, "My religion is better than your religion, and my pastor is better than your pastor." Paul negates any feasibility for bragging of spiritual achievement by defining its following points.

Sovereign Placement

A placement of person and task is assigned by God. "What, after all, is Apollos? And what is Paul? Only servants, through whom you came to believe—as the Lord has assigned to each his task" (1 Cor. 3:5). The pastor toils all year planting seed, and an evangelist comes along and reaps. No one ever accomplishes anything alone. We are debtors to those who labor before us, after us, and with us. We are debtors to *all* who have gone before us; some of us have had better predecessors than others. Because of these antecedents in our lives, a small accomplishment may be a greater miracle in one life than a large accomplishment in another.

As C. S. Lewis argued in another context, just because my teeth are yellow, you cannot accuse me of not brushing them, or that the toothpaste I am using is ineffective. You do not know what they would look like if I didn't brush them (Lewis 1952:163). This may translate into "When God chose me to be your pastor, you may not know with how little he began." God had a lot to work with when he chose Apollos, who was quite gifted, but as Paul wrote, "What after all is Apollos? And what is Paul? Only servants through whom you came to believe—as the Lord had assigned to each his task. I planted the seed, Apollos watered it" (1 Cor. 3:5–6). The circumstances of life are ordered by God as well as the gifts of grace. Even if a person says, "I chose this route," he or she must understand that even the ability to choose correctly is a gift of God's grace.

Sovereign Results

All success is from God, "but God made it grow. So neither he who plants nor he who waters is anything, but only God, who makes things grow" (1 Cor. 3:6, 7). Jesus said that it rains on the just and the unjust. Is it possible for rain to fall on the fields of the just while at the same time the soil of the unjust is being watered from heaven? It could be that there is some pastor who has been twice as diligent this year as someone else who received the denominational plaudits. He even may have been twice as spiritual. In fact, a relationship with persons may have been sacrificed for a relationship with God. Above all, self-aggrandizement and egotism must be sacrificed to the all-sufficiency of the Holy Spirit. After Samuel Logan Brengle, the Salvation Army Commissioner had been introduced as "the great Dr. Brengle," he penned in his diary:

> If I appear great in their eyes, the Lord is most graciously helping me to see how absolutely nothing I am without Him, and helping me to keep little in my own eyes. He does use me. But I am so concerned that He uses me and that it is not of me the work is done. The axe cannot boast of the trees it has cut down. It could do nothing but for the woodsman. He made it, he sharpened it, and he used it. The moment he throws it aside, it becomes only old iron. O that I may never lose sight of this (Hall 1933:275).

Team Effort

We're all in this thing together. We are not in a race to see who can stand alone at the top of the heap. "The man who plants and the man who waters have one purpose, and each will be rewarded according to his own labor" (1 Cor. 3:8). We are all on the same team, each with a unique place on the team, driving toward the same goal. Paul was so convinced of this that he believed common pursuit of the goal more important than discerning who was not playing by the rules, or who had ulterior motives not in the best interests of the team. "But what does it matter? The important thing is that in every way, whether from false motives or true, Christ is preached. And because of this I rejoice" (Phil. 1:18). My ability to rejoice in the success of others is an acid test of whether I have a team spirit, and whether my own achievements are sacrificed to the overall good of the team.

Works Sacrificed to Christ

There is only one basis or foundation on which to build the kingdom: the person of Jesus Christ. "For no one can lay any foundation other than the one already laid, which is Jesus Christ" (1 Cor. 3:11). There is not complete agreement on exactly what Paul meant here, but it seems from the context that he could not have meant a doctrine that was absolutely false, because it is plainly stated that the builder himself will be saved (v. 14). The distinction between costly stones and hay leads us to ask if there is a labor that is more valid than others, is there also a work that is superficial yet makes a fabulous show? We are reminded of that awesome eschatological confrontation of Christ with the seven churches in the Book of Revelation: "I know thy works." Is Christ saying, "I know you intimately. I know your motives, your faithfulness, and your intentions. I know why you work—you may be working more for yourself than for me. Has your work been crucified by my cross? Has your work been sanctified by the Holy Spirit?"

The foundation must be not only Christ but also Jesus Christ and him crucified. The cross is the quality-control factor for our works. They pale into insignificance in the light of Calvary. Only as they pale into insignificance because we are focused on Golgotha can they become significant for the kingdom. What a shame for a pastor to be egotistical and pompous. He is a great worker supposedly for the kingdom, but his work will not survive God's refining fire. Some egos become so inflated that their success actually destroys their eternal effectiveness. Spurgeon wrote:

> Success exposes a man to the pressure of people and this tempts him to hold on to his gain by means of fleshly methods and practices, and to let himself be ruled wholly by the dictatorial demands of incessant expansion. Success can go to my head and will unless I remember that it is God who accomplishes the work, that he can continue to do so without my help, and that he will be able to make out with other means when ever he cuts me down to size (quoted in Sanders 1980:231).

Tested by Fire

Awards day will be stringent. Recognition will be given only to those people who can survive fire. "His work will be shown for what it is, because the Day will bring it to light. It will be revealed with fire, and the fire will test the quality of each man's work. If what he has built survives, he will receive his reward" (1 Cor. 3:13–14). The evaluation of our life work will be in depth, done by the one who knows our thoughts from afar off, who knows when we sit down and when we stand up. God has truly searched us and known us, and his observations will come to light in the eschaton (Psalm 139). Perhaps the only way that our works will not be consumed in that day is for our hearts to be purged in this life.

Samuel Chadwick, when only twenty-one years old, was praying for revival in the small evangelical church he pastored at Stackstead, Lancashire. Very disciplined and studious, he had fifteen sermons in his "barrel" that he had carefully prepared and that had seemingly been blessed in revival campaigns elsewhere. Yet there was not renewal in his own church. At 3 A.M. one Sunday morning, the Holy Spirit suggested to him that he might be depending more on those sermons than on the power of Pentecost. Chadwick dropped his sermons into the fire and according to his own testimony, the fire of Pentecost visited his heart and life. Revival came to his church and often accompanied his preaching for the rest of his life. He referred to his personal Pentecost as his "ashes and fire" crisis. God will need to purge selfishness, vanity, egotism, envy, jealousy, lust, and all other attitudes and traits that taint ministry in this life so that it can withstand the fire of his judgment (Lown 1983:3).

Eternal versus Temporal Standards

God's standards for success are not man's standards. "For the wisdom of this world is foolishness in God's sight. As it is written: 'He catches the wise in their craftiness'; and again, 'The Lord knows that the thoughts of the wise are futile'" (1 Cor. 3:19–20). God's perception of our achievements is not necessarily our perception and vice versa. We tabulate the results while God examines the heart. The first demands minimum intelligence while the second requires infinite wisdom. The process of evaluating the faithfulness of ministry is so precarious that it is only of divine appointment. Paul wrote:

> I care very little if I am judged by you or by any human court; indeed, I do not even judge myself. My conscience is clear, but that does not make me innocent. It is the Lord who judges me. Therefore judge nothing before the appointed time; wait till the Lord comes. He will bring to light what is hidden in darkness and will expose the motives of men's hearts. At that time each will receive his praise from God (1 Cor. 4:3–5).

In the light of the above, how could any deed ever receive an unqualified stamp of success? More accurately, we should say, "From my perception, it went well, but God will have the final say." In 1 Corinthians 4, Paul does not use the simple word for passing judgment, *krino,* but *anakrino,* which connotes a more complex examination or investigation. It is an examination that can be done only in part by us in this life, because we see through a glass darkly. When God examines the motives of an individual and "brings to light what is hidden in darkness," there will no doubt be startling surprises. It was this kind of surprise that Dante expressed in his *Divine Comedy* when he toured the regions of the beyond:

> In judgment be ye not too confident,
> Even as a man who will appraise his corn
> When standing in a field, ere it is ripe
> For I have seen the briar show itself
> Stiff and intractable all winter long,
> Yet later bear the rose upon its stem.
> And once I saw a vessel, staunch and swift,
> Course o'er the sea for her entire voyage,
> Only to perish at the harbor's mouth.
> Let not Dame Bertha or old Martin think,
> When they see one man steal, another pray,
> That they perceive the heavenly counsels there:
> The former one may rise, the latter fall (Dante 1948:152).

A Legacy of Success

In A.D. 37, Damascus was an important stop for the trade caravans that traveled east and west. It had been a center of world commerce for hundreds of years, located approximately halfway between the civilizations of Egypt and Mesopotamia. Its language, Aramaic, was the vernacular spoken by both Jesus and Paul. It is no coincidence that a full-blooded Aramean, Ananias, completed their introduction to each other.

For centuries Damascus had been confronted by Judaism through both wars and alliances. At times Damascus was under the dominion of Israel. Even though she had thrown off Israel's rule, she had not thrown off its

religion. Thus, at the time of Jesus Christ, the predominant religion in the city was that of the Jewish syna-
gogue. Of course there were many other "gods" that
trailed through, and to the residents a new sect was just
another religion to roll down the pike.

But Ananias, as a devout Jew, knew enough Scripture
and walked closely enough to God to perceive the truth of
the Jesus story. He became a convert and began converting others to "The Way." With his small group of
Christians gathered around him, he became a marked
man. It could be that Ananias's house was used as a stop-
ping point for Christian tradesmen and he thus became a
chief disseminator of the good news. It may well have
been that he was number one on Paul's hit list as he traveled to Damascus: if Ananias could be quieted, a chief
link in Christians' communication would be severed.
Instead, Ananias became a seminal individual in the history of Christianity. Yet he is mentioned in only one context in the entirety of Scripture, the conversion of Paul.
He is the "one-touch person," and those who have followed in his train have possessed the "Ananias touch."

Had Ananias not been living so close to God that he
could obey instructions that were contrary to all reason,
we never would have heard his name. Had he not been
willing to cast aside bias and minister to a man about
whom he had heard much evil, his most important opportunity of evangelism would have been missed. It was
Ananias who explained the Christian way more fully to
Paul and who laid hands on him that he might be filled
with the Holy Spirit. But Ananias did not just send Paul
on his way; he took him in and introduced him to the
church gathered at Damascus. Though the church was
small and struggling, it would forever possess on its rolls
the best-known name of Christendom.

Because one man lived close to God, he perceived the
potential for good in another man. He was God's man, at
the right place, at the right time. Thus was Edward
Kimball when, one afternoon in a Boston shoe store, he

spoke to Dwight L. Moody about his relationship with Christ. Thus was Mordecai Ham when a young Billy Graham heard him preach almost a half century ago. Thus was a Methodist circuit rider whom James Taylor heard preach. James Taylor was the first of seven generations of Taylors to become fervent Christians and carry the gospel around the world. The best known of them was James Hudson Taylor, a monument in the history of missions. The influence of that itinerant Methodist preacher who ignited an unbroken zeal continues over two hundred years later, though his name has been lost to history.

There are thousands of other names, lost forever, of men and women who with small gifts labored in small vineyards. Just because those vineyards were small, God did not deny them a harvester. In the small harvest was a man or woman who would touch the lives of multitudes around the globe. The legacy of the Ananias touch is multiplied a thousand times. The task was hard, the hours long, the pay scarce, and the rewards few, but the Ananiases of history have faithfully labored in obscurity. Their effectiveness will come to light in another world.

In 1920 a young man from Japan named David Tsutada boarded a passenger ship bound for London (Tsutada 1971:4). He had been raised in a Christian home by well-to-do parents. Even though he had been taken to church and taught the Scriptures, he had never experienced justification by faith and the assurance of salvation. On board the ship was a young man named John Owen Gauntlett who became a steadfast friend of David's. John did some probing concerning David's spiritual condition and found that his friend was floating on a sea of uncertainty.

After arriving in London, David, a student in law school on a Rhodes Scholarship, and John, a theological student, continued their relationship, meeting once a week to discuss spiritual matters. One afternoon, after John had pressed the matter of personal salvation, David knelt in a corner of his small dormitory room and entered into a permanent relationship with Jesus Christ. One month before graduation from law school, he dropped out and returned to Japan to start a church.

David Tsutada endured much persecution at the hands of his countrymen during World War II. He was imprisoned in solitary confinement because he pledged unreserved allegiance to Jesus Christ instead of the emperor. On being released from prison, he was so malnourished that he could not even speak, but eventually he continued to preach Christ and establish churches. Today David Tsutada is no longer living, but as a result of his labors and those who followed him, there are twelve thousand members of the Japan Immanuel General Missions's 110 churches, the largest indigenous Christian denomination in Japan. Their discipleship is traced directly to the witness of one man to another. John Gauntlett put a boat ride to its best possible use by sharing Jesus Christ with a fellow traveler.

Ananiases continue to put boat rides, plane rides, whatever they are doing, wherever they are going, wherever they are, to their best possible use. They pray as they go, "God, there isn't much going on here and I don't see much happening, but you must have put me here for a purpose. I'm determined to make the best of the opportunity. I'm a common man, living in a common place, a common street, a street called Straight. Help me not to miss the potential John Calvins, Martin Luthers, John Wesleys, and David Tsutadas who pass by. If I do, I will fail you, fail the world, and fail the kingdom of God."

Conclusion

Paul throughout his writings presents a case for successful ministry. Success is based on principles of character rather than tangible, measurable results. He was not reticent to remind the Ephesian leaders of the kind of person he had been: trustworthy, empathetic, sanctified, and Spirit filled. It is true that Paul planted many churches and seemingly had hundreds of converts, but we do not know that he ever built an edifice. We do not know what the annual budget was of any church in which he was pastor. What we do know is that the people he left behind were better people because he had been with them. Will that be true of us? Though not easily calculable, such a question is worthwhile for any pastor to ask after he preaches his final sermon to a congregation of believers.

Afterword
A Final Reflection
on Pastoral Success

Jesus said, "I am the good shepherd. The good shepherd lays down his life for the sheep" (John 10:11). He lays down his life with unconditional love and without false motives. A good shepherd leads the sheep, feeds the sheep, protects the sheep, and sacrifices for the sheep. He knows the sheep individually and is known by the sheep. Skilled shepherds attempt to do all the right things so that the sheep under their care will reach their maximum potential as sheep, that they will become good wool-producing, meat-providing, or reproducing sheep.

Many and possibly all of the men we interviewed for this study are sacrificial shepherds, expending long hours and high energy for the welfare of their people. They are doing all in their power and perception to see that their people are becoming mature, fruit-bearing Christians. Through their ministry, quality spiritual life is being realized in large numbers of people. To whatever extent Christ-likeness is being formed in their flock, they are successful. If their motives are other than what they should be, God will be the judge. Some men's sins will go before them, some after (1 Tim. 5:24). And we should be quite hesitant to criticize a person who is pointing others to Christ. Paul wrote, "The important thing is that in every way, whether from false motives or true, Christ is preached. And because of this I rejoice" (Phil. 1:18).

Even if Jesus meant for shepherding to provide a central paradigm for ministry, he certainly understood that people are more complicated than sheep and being a minister is more complicated than shepherding. Spiritual qualities ignited within people are more difficult to assess than fine wool and savory mutton. More essential than the shepherd's skill in feeding the sheep is that the sheep know the shepherd. Feeling and following the heart of the master shepherd is the true measure of the undershepherd's greatness.

But even though pastoral skills are much more complex than shepherding, perhaps Jesus was suggesting that the principles of success for each are not all that different. An individual under the call of God gives himself wholeheartedly, according to God-given wisdom but limited perception, by the power of the Holy Spirit to the spiritual nurture of people. That is success, whatever the measurable results. And if sheep can discern that the shepherd is for them, certainly people can sense that a spiritual leader is laboring with their best interests in mind. Long hours, crisis ministry in the middle of the night, and conscientious faithfulness to day-by-day tasks spell sacrifice. The pastor's example underscores the message that he preaches: love of God and compassion for others. His ability to both rejoice with others and weep with them says that people are important. It says, "I am willing to put others' needs ahead of mine." No greater love than this, that a man lay down his life for others, translates into success at its deepest level and meaning.

Though we have argued for common denominators, the actual deeds and preparation for those deeds will be as varied as are the men and their pastoral settings. For that reason, imitating a successful sheep herder will be more profitable than imitating a successful pastor. In fact, the latter will probably end in defeat. Victory will come only because Christ has complete control of the pastor's life. This means doing God's will in God's way in God's time. That's the way Christ pleased the Father.

Pleasing the Godhead is the most succinct essence of success, whether a person be a pastor, baker, butcher, or candlestick maker.

Even after reading these pages, there may be those who are uneasy about the word *success,* especially as it relates to ministry. The uneasiness is well founded, especially if success connotes merit or inherent worth outside of God's grace. One cannot too often heed Zechariah's reminder that "Not by might, nor by power, but by my spirit, saith the LORD of hosts" (Zech. 4:6).

On the other hand, success can be defined as a job well done. These two perspectives—giving my best, and total reliance on God—render success paradoxical. The results are left up to God, but the pastor has given himself to attaining the best results possible, both quantitative and qualitative. He can come to the end of his ministry with integrity rather than despair. In the words of Erikson, "He has taken care of things and people" (Erikson 1963:168).

Some readers may be uneasy about the simplicity of Christ's ministry contrasted to our detailed investigation of ministerial qualities and effectiveness. The gap is partially explained by the uniqueness of Christ's mission and the cultural parameters within which he worked. On the other hand, I do not find contradiction between Christ's ministry and the ingredients of modern ministry I have identified. Christ had an inclusive personality that was enticing; at the same time, he did not ignore the evils of his day.

All Christians face the tension between separation and identification. The tension is further strained for the pastor who has to decide which twenty-first-century secular means should be used in a sacred cause. The pastor in this dilemma may find solace and direction in Paul's words, "To the pure, all things are pure" (Titus 1:15).

It is encouraging and inspiring to take a close look at any group of people who give themselves wholeheartedly to the task at hand. Mediocrity is a blight on any profession. There are those in every calling who do their best to escape mediocrity. This study has attempted to define who, what, and why they are among those who practice parish ministry as a lifelong vocation. If any occupation is worthy of the best a person has to give, it is being a pastor. We are indebted to the persons who have set that model before us. The world is a better place for them.

Endnotes

Chapter 1

1. There was no one person who fit the above description. We are creating a proto-pastor from the survey data. For instance, in determining management style, all of the top choices were considered to determine a composite profile. The second, third, and fourth choices were not blended into the picture. To arrive at an average profile, the percentage within each category would have to be averaged for each person.

2. Only 6 percent of our respondents served as associate pastors, while 20 percent were the founding pastors.

3. About 33 percent perceived themselves as extroverted-rationalistic and 43 percent as extroverted-intuitive. Almost 17 percent saw themselves as introverted-rationalistic or intuitive.

4. 28 percent Dominant, 23 percent Inducive, 36 percent Steady, 3 percent Compliant, 5 percent combination or hedged. See McManus, 1978.

Bibliography

Ahlstrom, Sydney E. *A Religious History of the American People*. New Haven: Yale University Press, 1975.

Albright, Raymond W. *Focus on Infinity*. New York: The Macmillan Company, 1961.

Allport, Gordon W. *The Individual and His Religion*. New York: The Macmillan Company, 1950.

Barrett, David B. *Evangelize! A Historical Survey of the Concept*. Birmingham: New Hope, 1987.

Bauer, Walter, William E. Arndt, and F. Wilbur Gingrich. *A Greek-English Lexicon of the New Testament*. Chicago: University of Chicago Press, 1979.

Baumann, J. Daniel. *An Introduction to Contemporary Preaching*. Grand Rapids: Baker Book House, 1972.

Baxter, Richard. *The Reformed Pastor*. Abridged by Thomas Rutherford. New York: Carlton & Lanahan, n.d.

Bellah, Robert N. et al., eds. *Habits of the Heart*. New York: Harper and Row, 1985.

Berger, Peter L. *A Rumor of Angels*. Garden City, N.Y.: Doubleday & Company, 1969.

Blackwood, Andrew W. *Pastoral Work*. Grand Rapids: Baker Book House, 1971.

Blizzard, Samuel E. "The Protestant Parish Minister: A Behavioral Science Interpretation." *Society for the Scientific Study of Religion*, 1985.

Blotnick, Srully. *Ambitious Men*. New York: Viking Penguin, Inc., 1987.

Borg, Marcus J. *Jesus: A New Vision*. San Francisco: Harper and Row, 1987.

Bosley, Harold A. "The Role of Preaching in American History," pp. 17–35 in DeWitte Holland, ed., *Preaching in American History*. Nashville: Abingdon Press, 1969.

Brown, Francis, S. R. Driver, and Charles A. Briggs. *A Hebrew and English Lexicon of the Old Testament*. London: Oxford University Press, 1972.

Bruce, F. F. *Paul: Apostle of the Heart Set Free*. Grand Rapids: Eerdmans, 1977.

Callan, Terrence. "Competition and Boasting: Towards a Psychological Portrait of Paul." *Journal of Religious Studies*, 13, No. 2, 27–51.

Capps, Donald, et al., eds. *Encounter with Erikson*. Missoula, MT: Scholars Press, 1977.

Chambers, Oswald. *The Best from all His Books*, Nashville: Thomas Nelson, 1987.

Carlyle, Thomas. *Heroes and Hero Worship*. New York: The Macmillan Company, 1910.

Collins, Jr. Edward M. "The Rhetoric of Sensation Challenges the Rhetoric of the Intellect: An Eighteenth Century Controversy," pp. 98–117 in *Preaching in American History,* DeWitte Holland, ed. Nashville: Abingdon, 1969.

Constitutions of the Holy Apostles, in Vol. 7 of the *Ante-Nicene Fathers*. New York: Charles Scribner's Sons, 1913.

Dallimore, Arnold. *Spurgeon*. Chicago: Moody Press, 1984.

Dante Alighieri. *The Divine Comedy*. New York: Pantheon Books, 1948.

Dayton, Donald W. *Theological Roots of Pentecostalism*. Grand Rapids: Zondervan, 1987.

Dunning, Norman G. *The Story of Samuel Chadwick*. Salem, OH: Convention Book Store, 1971.

Dvorak, Katherine L. "Peter Cartwright and Charisma." *Methodist History*, XXVI, No. 2 (Jan. 1988), 113–126.

Engel, James F. *Contemporary Christian Communications*. Nashville: Thomas Nelson Publishers, 1979.

Erikson, Erik H. *Childhood and Society,* 2nd ed. New York: W. W. Norton & Company, 1963.

_____. *Gandhi's Truth*. New York: W. W. Norton & Company, 1969.

_____. *Identity: Youth and Crisis*. New York: W. W. Norton & Company, 1968.

_____. *Insight and Responsibility*. New York: W. W. Norton & Company, 1964.

_____. *Life History and the Historical Moment*. New York: W. W. Norton & Company, 1975.

_____. *Young Man Luther*. New York: W. W. Norton & Company, 1962.

Ferguson, Charles W. *Organizing to Beat the Devil*. Garden City, NY: Doubleday and Company, 1971.

Finney, Charles G. *Memoirs of the Rev. Charles G. Finney.* London: Hodder and Staughton, 1876.

Firet, Jacob. *Dynamics of Pastoring.* Grand Rapids: Wm. B. Eerdmans Publishing Company, 1986.

Friedman, Meyer and Ray H. Rosenman. *Type A Behavior and Your Heart.* New York: Alfred A. Knopf, Inc., 1974.

Friedrich, Gerhard. *Theological Dictionary of the New Testament,* Vol. 5. Grand Rapids: Wm. B. Eerdmans Publishing Company, 1967.

Gasque, W. Ward. "The Church in Search of Excellence" (Book Review of *In Search of Excellence*). *Christianity Today,* Feb. 15, 1985, 54–6.

Glasse, James D. *Putting it Together in the Parish.* Nashville: Abingdon Press, 1972.

Gregory the Great. "Book of Pastoral Rule," *The Nicene and Post-Nicene Fathers,* Vol. 13. Grand Rapids: Wm. B. Eerdmans Publishing Co., 1956.

Grounds, Vernon. "Faith for Failure: A Meditation on Motivation for Ministry." *TSF Bulletin,* Mar–Apr 1986, pp. 3–5.

Guthrie, Donald. *New Testament Introduction.* Downers Grove, IL: InterVarsity Press, 1970.

Haines, T. L., and Yaggy, L. W. *The Royal Path of Life.* Chicago: Western Publishing House, 1876.

Hall, Clarence W. *Samuel Logan Brengle: Portrait of a Prophet.* New York: The Salvation Army, 1933.

Halverson, Richard C. *How I Changed My Thinking About the Church.* Grand Rapids: Zondervan, 1972.

Harris, R. Laird, Gleason L. Archer, Jr., and Bruce K Waltke, eds. *Theological Wordbook of the Old Testament.* Chicago: Moody Press, 1980.

Hatch, Nathan. "Evangelicalism as a Democratic Movement" in *Evangelicalism and Modern America,* George Marsden, ed. Grand Rapids: Wm. B. Eerdmans Publishing Company, 1984.

Hibben, Paxton. *Henry Ward Beecher: An American Portrait.* New York: The Press of the Readers Club, 1942.

Hickman, Craig R. and Michael A. Silva. *The Future 500.* New York: NAL Books, 1987.

Hills, A. M. *Life of Martin Wells Knapp.* Noblesville, IN: Newby Book Room, 1973.

Holifield, E. Brooks. *A History of Pastoral Care in America.* Nashville: Abingdon Press, 1983.

Holmes, William A. "Called to be Faithful—Not Big or Small." *Circuit Rider,* June 1987, pp. 5–6.

Howard, Ivan Cushing. *Controversies in Methodism over Methods of Education of Ministers up to 1865.* Unpublished Ph.D. dissertation, University of Iowa, 1965.

Hudson, Wintrop. "The Ministry in the Puritan Age" in *The Ministry in Historical Perspective.* H. Richard Niebuhr and Daniel D. Williams, eds. New York: Harper and Brothers, 1956.

Hunter, James Davison. *American Evangelicalism.* New Brunswick, NJ: Rutgers University Press, 1983.

Jacobsen, Wayne. "The Numbers Game: A Threat to Churches Large and Small." *Leadership,* Winter 1983, pp. 49–53.

Jowett, J. H. *The Preacher: His Life and Work.* Garden City, NY: Doubleday, Doran & Company, 1928.

Jung, Carl. *The Portable Jung,* Joseph Campbell, ed. New York: The Viking Press, 1971.

Kavanaugh, John Francis. *Following Christ in a Consumer Society.* Maryknoll, NY: Orbis Books, 1981.

Kelley, Dean M. *Why Conservative Churches Are Growing.* New York: Harper & Row, 1972.

Kierkegaard, Sören. *Fear and Trembling.* Garden City, NY: Doubleday Anchor Books, 1954.

Kinlaw, Dennis F. *Preaching in the Spirit.* Grand Rapids: Zondervan, 1985.

Küng, Hans. *The Church.* Garden City, NY: Image Books, 1976.

Lake, Frank. *Clinical Theology.* London: Darton, Longman & Todd, 1966.

Laurence, William. "The Relation of Wealth to Morals," in *Christian Social Teachings,* George W. Forell, ed. Minneapolis, MN: Augsburg Publishing House, 1966.

"Leadership Forum. Must a Healthy Church be a Growing Church?" pp. 127–138 in *Leadership.* Vol. II, No. 1, Winter 1981.

Lewis, C. S. *Mere Christianity.* New York: The Macmillan Company, 1952.

Lown, Albert J. "And they were Filled with the Spirit." *The Sounding Board,* Vol. I, No. 4 (Spring 1983), passim.

Maccoby, Michael. "Leadership Needs of the 1980's." *Current Issues in Higher Education,* No. 1, 1979, pp. 17–22.

MacLaren, Alexander. *The Victor's Crowns.* New York: Funk & Wagnals Company, 1902.

Martin, Enos. "Depression in the Clergy." *Leadership,* Winter 1982, pp. 81–9.

McManus, Leo F. *Participant Manual for Management and Motivation.* Worcester, MA: L. F. McManus Company, 1978.

Mead, Sidney E. "Denominationalism: The Shape of Protestantism in America." In *Denominationalism,* Russell E. Richey, ed. Nashville: Abingdon Press, 1977, pp. 70–105.

____. "The Rise of the Evangelical Conception of the Ministry in America: 1607–1850." In *The Ministry in Historical Perspectives,* H. Richard Niebuhr and Daniel D. Williams, eds. New York: Harper and Brothers, 1956, pp. 207–49.

Menninger, Karl. *Whatever Became of Sin?* New York: Hawthorn Books, Inc., 1793.

Muggeridge, Malcolm. *Jesus Rediscovered.* Garden City, NY: Doubleday, 1969.

Myers, Isabel Briggs and Mary H. McCaulley. *Manual: A Guide to the Development and Use of the Myers-Briggs Type Indicator.* Palo Alto, CA: Consulting Psychologists Press, 1985.

Naisbett, John. *Megatrends.* New York: Warner Books, 1982.

Niebuhr, H. Richard. *The Purpose of the Church and Its Ministry.* New York: Harper & Brothers, 1956.

Niebuhr, Reinhold, *The Irony of American History.* New York: Charles Scribner's Sons, 1952.

____. *Leaves from the Notebook of a Tamed Cynic.* New York: Meridian Books, 1957.

____. *The Nature and Destiny of Man,* Vol. 1. New York: Charles Scribner's Sons, 1964.

Norwood, Frederick A. *The Story of American Methodism.* Nashville: Abingdon Press, 1974.

Novak, Michael. *The Joy of Sports.* New York: Basic Books, Inc., 1976.

Oden, Thomas. *Crisis Ministries.* New York: Crossroad Publishing Company, 1983.

____. *Game Free: A Guide to the Meaning of Intimacy.* New York: Harper and Row, 1974.

____. *Kerygma and Counseling.* Philadelphia: The Westminster Press, 1966.

____. *Pastoral Theology.* San Francisco: Harper and Row, 1983.

Packer, J. I. *Evangelism & the Sovereignty of God.* Downers Grove, IL: InterVarsity Press, 1961.

Peck, M. Scott. *The Road Less Traveled.* New York: Simon and Schuster, 1978.

Peters, Thomas J. and Robert H. Waterman, Jr. *In Search of Excellence.* New York: Warner Books, 1982.

Poritt, Arthur. *John Henry Jowett.* New York: George H. Doran Company, 1925.

Posey, Walter Brownlow. *Frontier Mission.* Lexington, KY: University of Kentucky Press, 1966.

Posner, Mitchell J. *Executive Essentials.* New York: Avon Books, 1982.

R.I.S.E. "Initial Findings of an Institutional and Contextual Analysis of the Santa Clara County." San Jose: Research in Strategic Evangelization, 1986.

Robinson, Haddon W. *Biblical Preaching.* Grand Rapids: Baker Book House, 1980.

Sager, Allan H. "The Fundamentalist-Modernist Controversy: 1918-1930" pp. 258-77 in *Preaching in American History,* DeWitte Holland, ed. Nashville: Abingdon Press, 1969.

Sanders, J. Oswald. *Spiritual Leadership*, rev. ed. Chicago: Moody Press, 1980.

Schaller, Lyle E. "Is Pastoral Ministry a Personality Cult?" *The Clergy Journal,* Feb. 1987, pp. 34-5.

Schoenstein, Ralph. "I Hear America Polling." *Newsweek,* Oct. 10, 1983.

Schorr, Henry. *Senior Pastor Needs for Preparatory and Continuing Professional Education as Perceived by Seminary Professors.* Unpublished Ph.D. dissertation, 1984.

Scott, Donald M. *From Office to Profession.* Philadelphia: University of Pennsylvania Press, 1978.

Smith, Donald P. *Congregations Alive.* Philadelphia: The Westminster Press, 1981.

Stein, Michelle. "'Shopping Center Church' Stocks Shelves with TLC." *The Oregonian,* Oct. 27, 1987.

Stout, Harry. *The New England Soul.* New York: Oxford University Press, 1986.

Structure of Ministry. South Barrington, IL: Willow Creek Community Church.

Telford, John. *The Life of John Wesley.* London: The Epworth Press, 1953.

Tillapaugh, Frank R. *The Church Unleashed.* Ventura, CA: Regal Books, 1982.

Towns, Elmer L., et al. *The Complete Book of Church Growth.* Wheaton, IL: Tyndale House, 1981.

Tozer, A. W. *The Best of A. W. Tozer,* compiled by Warren Wiersbe. Grand Rapids: Baker Book House, 1978.

____. *Man: The Dwelling Place of God.* Harrisburg, PA: Christian Publications, 1966.

Trueblood, D. Elton. "A Time for Holy Dissatisfaction: An Interview with D. Elton Trueblood." *Leadership,* Winter 1983, pp. 18–27.

Tsutada, David T. "Truth Does Not Change." *Decision,* 12, 1971, pp. 4, 13.

Vine, W. E. *Vine's Expository Dictionary of Biblical Words.* Nashville: Thomas Nelson Publishers, 1985.

Webster's Ninth New Collegiate Dictionary. Springfield, MA: Merriam-Webster, Inc., 1985.

Weisberger, Bernard A. *They Gathered at the River.* Boston: Little, Brown and Company, 1958.

Wesley, John. *The Journal of the Rev. John Wesley, A. M., Vol. IV.* Nehemiah Curnock, ed. London: The Epworth Press, 1938.

____. *The Letters of the Rev. John Wesley, A. M. Vol. IV.* John Telford, ed. London: The Epworth Press, 1931.

____. *Wesley's 52 Standard Sermons.* N. Burnwash, ed. Salem, Ohio: Convention Book Store, 1967.

____. *The Works of John Wesley, Vol. XII: Letters.* Grand Rapids: Zondervan, 1958.

____. *The Works of John Wesley, Vol. VIII.* Grand Rapids: Zondervan, 1958.

Whitmont, Edward C. *The Symbolic Quest.* Princeton, NJ: Princeton University Press, 1969.

Willimon, William H. and Robert L. Wilson. *Rekindling the Flame.* Nashville: Abingdon Press, 1987.

____. *Worship as Pastoral Care.* Nashville: Abingdon Press, 1979.

Winslow, Ola Elizabeth. *Jonathan Edwards.* New York: Octagon Books, 1973.

Wood, A. Skevington. *The Burning Heart.* Minneapolis, MN: Bethany Fellowship, 1978.